T0150665

LAKE GAR DA

MARCO POLO
TOP HIGHLIGHTS

FUNIVIA MALCESINE-MONTE BALDO ⭐1
The views from the scenic cable car and the 2,000-m-high peak are breathtaking.

➤ p. 57, Northern Shore

ARENA DI VERONA ⭐2
Even if opera is not your thing, you should definitely watch the open-air spectacle in the Roman arena once in your lifetime!
📷 *Tip: In the early morning, the piazza in front of the arena is empty and the light is at its best.*

➤ p. 82, Eastern Shore

STRADA DELLA FORRA ⭐4
The breathtaking scenic road leads from Pieve down to the lake.
📷 *Tip: Drive on this road in the evening when the illuminated gorges make perfect night-time pictures.*

➤ p. 116, Western Shore,
p. 127, Discovery Tours

PUNTA SAN VIGILIO ⭐3
One of the most beautiful places on the lake.
📷 *Tip: At sunset, the walls and windows of the Locanda San Vigilio take on a red glow.*

➤ p. 69, Eastern Shore

MUSEO DELLE SCIENZE MUSE IN TRENTO ⭐5
Experience alpine nature, glaciers, the creation of the Dolomites, a tropical greenhouse and much more over seven floors.

➤ p. 124, Discovery Tours

CASTELLO DI ARCO ⭐ 8

The castle perches like an eagle's nest on the 300-m-high rock.

📷 *Tip: The viewing platform halfway up is made of glass so that, in photographs, it looks as if you are floating.*

➤ p. 54, Northern Shore

VITTORIALE DEGLI ITALIANI ⭐ 9

Park, mausoleum and home of poet D'Annunzio: a bizarre collection of curiosities.

📷 *Tip: The porthole windows in the Schifamondo wing frame the Lake Garda panorama.*

➤ p. 109, Western Shore

PIAZZA GIACOMO MATTEOTTI ⭐ 6

In the evening, holidaymakers and local people alike stroll in this square in Bardolino that reaches down to the lake.

➤ p. 72, Eastern Shore

ROCCA SCALIGERA ⭐ 7

Enjoy the amazing views from the parapets of Sirmione's moated castle and across the roofs of the Old Town (photo).

➤ p. 88, Southern Shore

GIARDINO BOTANICO ANDRÉ HELLER ⭐ 10

This unusual park houses wonderful works of art by famous artists.

➤ p. 108, Western Shore

CONTENTS

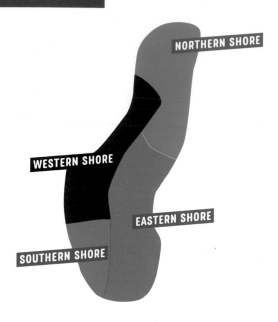

NORTHERN SHORE

WESTERN SHORE

EASTERN SHORE

SOUTHERN SHORE

CONTENTS

☉	Plan your visit	🍴	Eating & drinking		Rainy day activities
€–€€€	Price categories	🛍	Shopping		Budget activities
(*)	Premium-rate phone number	☿	Going out		Family activities
			Top beaches	⚑	Classic experiences

(□ A2) Refers to the removable pull-out map
(0) Located off the map

BEST OF LAKE GARDA

The Isola del Garda is only accessible on a guided tour

BEST ☂

WHEN IT RAINS

ACTIVITIES TO BRIGHTEN YOUR DAY

BOULDERING UNDER A ROOF

When it rains, climbers can still get their adrenalin kick at *Campfour Boulder* in Pietramurata. The bouldering centre has 500m² of climbing walls that are up to 5m high and multiple routes, so there is always something for everyone.
➤ p. 32, Sport & activities

VARONE WATERFALL

Regardless of the weather, the *Cascata del Varone*, created by the Tenno stream, sends a veil of spray into this narrow gorge. "A hellish spectacle" noted German novelist Thomas Mann.
➤ p. 48, Northern Shore

A VISIT TO THE WINE MUSEUM

The ideal place to learn about wine and try a drop or two is the *Museo del Vino* of the Cantina Zeni in Bardolino. It offers a glimpse into the intricacies of winemaking in the Verona region, from vine cultivation to bottle filling.
➤ p. 73, Eastern Shore

THE PATH OF THE WATER

At *Sea Life Gardaland*, visitors can trace the course of the water from a mountain stream through Lake Garda and the Po River delta to the Mediterranean Sea and the ocean. Sea horses swim alongside corals and sharks in the aquarium.
➤ p. 79, Eastern Shore

CITY TRIP

It's not difficult to keep out of the rain on a trip to *Verona*: visit any of its many museums, its famous churches such as San Zeno, and all sorts of inviting shops. You can drift from one boutique to the next along the Via Mazzini.
➤ p. 81, Eastern Shore

SAY CHEESE!

The *Alpe del Garda* dairy in Tremosine produces enough cheese to keep you smiling. Those who are interested can join a tour and, on request, a cheese tasting. Delicious!
➤ p. 116, Western Shore

BEST ON A BUDGET

FOR SMALLER WALLETS

APERITIF WITH SNACKS

With a Spritz (photo) or a glass of spumante in your hand, you can end the day in true Italian style. The best place to go is one of the classic aperitif bars that offer delicious and filling snacks free with a drink.

CURIOSITIES & CULTURE

Is the Aril the shortest river in the world? Its source is in Cassone near Malcesine and it flows into the lake after a leisurely 175m. Cassone harbour has the small, carefully curated fishing museum, *Museo del Lago*. Admission free!
➤ p. 59, Northern Shore

BARGAINS FOR OUTDOOR ENTHUSIASTS

Do you love climbing, hiking, mountain biking or camping? Mountaineering and outdoor clothing at discount prices can be found at the *Salewa Outlet* in Bussolengo.
➤ p. 81, Eastern Shore

TERRACE OF THRILL

Impressive mountain scenery rises high above the northwestern shore of the lake. To enjoy some amazing panoramic views you should travel to Tremosine. In nearby Pieve, stand on *Terrazza del Brivido*, the "Terrace of thrill", at the Hotel Paradiso and gaze into the depths; then order a cappuccino and relax.
➤ p. 116, Western Shore

CARD WITH DISCOUNTS!

With the *Garda Promotions Card* you receive discounts for numerous attractions, such as amusement parks, museums and ferry rides. It is available free of charge at many hotels or from tourist information offices.
➤ p. 137, Good to know

BEST WITH CHILDREN

FUN FOR YOUNG & OLD

CLIMBING ADVENTURE

In the *Elias Adventure Park* children can climb rocks and traverse high-rope courses. If you still have energy to spare, enjoy the "Flying Fox", a 200-m-long zip-line that stretches across the park and the River Sarca.
➤ p. 54, Northern Shore

FUN FOR ALL THE FAMILY

Sail on board a ship past pirate villages, view mammoths from a train or explore the fairytale castle of the Prezzemolo dinodog: no one will be bored in the *Gardaland* theme park (photo)!
➤ p. 79, Eastern Shore

PARCO NATURA VIVA

Who said that you have to go to Africa for a safari? From the safety of your car, You can watch rhinoceroses, lions and tigers roaming free, in *Parco Natura Viva* safari park, located between Pastrengo and Bussolengo.
➤ p. 79, Eastern Shore

FLUFFY FRIENDS

Children can stroke sheep and donkeys on the teaching farm of the *Parco Giardino Sigurtà*. The maze challenges both the young and the old to find their way out!
➤ p. 81, Eastern Shore

NATURE HANDS ON

Watch flying dinosaur skeletons, touch blocks of ice and stroke stuffed animals – the natural science *Museo delle Scienze MuSe* in Trento is anything but a dusty old collection. Here, children can experience science hands on. Perfect for rainy summer days! Just be aware that this museum is popular and can get crowded.
➤ p. 124, Discovery Tours

BEST ⚑
CLASSIC EXPERIENCES

ONLY ON LAKE GARDA

MOUNTAIN PARADISE
Outdoor enthusiasts can be found on *Monte Baldo* – either racing downhill on mountain bikes, hiking to the summit or skiing down the slopes.
➤ p. 33, Sport & activities, p. 57, Northern Shore

ALPINE MEETS MEDITERRANEAN
Between Riva and Torbole (e.g. at the *Bar alla Sega*) you can enjoy sitting beneath the palm and oleander trees sipping a cappuccino or aperitif, while you appreciate the wonderful backdrop of the 2,000-m-high mountains.
➤ p. 50, Northern Shore

A BEAUTY PAGEANT FOR CASTLES
The powerful Scaliger family of Verona ruled over the eastern shore for centuries. In the 13th and 14th centuries they built *castles* in Malcesine (photo), Torri del Benaco and Sirmione.
➤ p. 55, Northern Shore, p. 64, Eastern Shore, p. 88, Southern Shore

SEDUCTIVE FLORA
The fragrance of lemon trees, bougainvillea and rosemary is all pervasive. You can buy these plants in the *Flover Garden Centre* in Bussolengo, but to see Alpine species visit the *Orto Botanico del Monte Baldo*.
➤ p. 71 and p. 81, Eastern Shore

A GLASS OF BARDOLINO
The vineyards that produce Bardolino wine are on the slopes above the village of the same name. You can sample and buy wine directly from the producers, e.g. at *Cantine Lenotti*.
➤ p. 74, Eastern Shore

TAKE TO THE WATER!
Take to the water to see how beautifully the villages snuggle into the hills along the lakeside. And whoever wants to explore the opposite side of the lake can simply take *a ferry* between Torri and Toscolano.
➤ p. 134, Getting around

GET TO KNOW LAKE GARDA

"What's up?" A friendly cow at Monte Baldo

DISCOVER LAKE GARDA

La Montanara in Riva's Old Town serves rustic Trentino cuisine

Long pebble beaches and snowy mountain peaks, palm trees and holm oaks: Lake Garda has myriad natural attractions – and visitors will discover their own favourite aspect of its unique charm. It offers guests a taste of the Mediterranean lifestyle where people can enjoy *la dolce vita.*

Those who have been spellbound by the *lago* will return time and again. Why? Well, perhaps it's because of the wonderful *centri storici*, the palms, the cypress trees or olive groves. Or maybe it's the many castles and picturesque harbours.Or possibly it's the fruity ice cream and quaffable red wine. In all honesty, it's most likely to be a combination of all those elements. At the same time, the lake is large enough (at 370km²) to satisfy those cravings for a beach holiday. Well, almost: at its widest point, the lake measures a mere 17km … However, with that first glass of Spritz in your hand, you will soon feel as if you are lounging by the Mediterranean.

15 BCE
The Romans arrive at the lake and name it *Benacus*

1260-1387
The Scaligers rule in Verona and on the lake

1387-1405
The Milanese Visconti family rules over the Lake Garda region

1405-1797
The Venetians take control of the eastern shore

1797
The western shore is taken over by Napoleon while the eastern shore goes to Austria

1821-1861
Risorgimento period: the movement for a united Italy. In 1861, Italy becomes a

PEACE & QUIET ON THE WESTERN SHORE

The northern side of the lake is quite different from the south, and the same goes for the eastern and western shores. These contrasts give the lake its special atmosphere. Halfway down the western shore it is extremely peaceful. If you are content to simply read a paper or a book, and to hear nothing other than the flapping of sails in the wind, Gargnano is the place for you. Art nouveau villas and exclusive hotels are to be found around this part of the lake. In the late 19th century, Austrian hotelier Louis Wimmer recognized the charm of Lake Garda and built the first grand hotel in Gardone. Others soon followed.

THE LIVELY EASTERN SHORE

In contrast, the eastern shore has a younger, livelier vibe – but is just as picturesque. If you like shopping and eating out, Bardolino and Garda will suit you. The little lanes of the old towns can be more crowded in the evenings than during the day, and you will see children running around holding ice creams until midnight. If you're up for a real taste of nightlife, then head to the southern shore. Some of the biggest clubs in and around Desenzano are popular with night-owls from the entire region.

PURE ADVENTURE

The north of the lake is surrounded by high peaks, up to 2,000m, deep valleys and steep walls of rock, making it the perfect destination for outdoor sports

sovereign nation

1919
After World War I, Lake Garda is entirely Italian territory

1943–1945
The Republic of Salò is formed under dictator Benito Mussolini

1946
Italy becomes a Republic

1962
The cable car from Malcesine to the peak of Monte Baldo opens

2013
The MuSe, Italy's largest museum of natural sciences, opens in Trento

2018
The first leg of the Lake Garda bike path opens at Limone

enthusiasts. Adventure-lovers try their luck canyoning and exploring otherwise inaccessible ravines accompanied by mountain guides; mountain bikers and hikers roam the mountain slopes; climbers ascend the rugged rock faces and are sometimes suspended directly over the lake. For water-sports fans, Lake Garda's reliable winds between Limone, Riva del Garda and Malcesine make this one of Europe's ideal locations for sailing Fifty years ago, it was mainly windsurfers and sailors who floated across the waves; today the lake is also popular with kitesurfers, stand-up paddleboarders and kayakers. Water-skiing and parasailing are popular too, although mainly in the south, as motorboats are not allowed in the north.

The further south you travel – where the shoreline is wider, and occasionally there's even a sandy beach – the more crowded things get, especially during the hot summer months. If you don't like the hustle and bustle, you can enjoy watching the sunset at a picturesque jetty – for example in Cassone near Malcesine – and ignore the hubbub with an aperitif in your hand. Or you can explore the hinterland; even regular visitors to Lake Garda discover new and exciting places for excursions.

VILLAS & ROMAN RUINS

Lake Garda is not just a paradise for sports lovers and sun worshippers. Famous guests such as Goethe, Nietzsche or Kafka once hunted for art treasures here. Today, interested visitors will also find a variety of cultural destinations. For example, the harmonious Romanesque church of San Severo in Bardolino or the Roman villa of Grotte di Catullo in Sirmione. A particularly enjoyable alternative is a kayak or canoe tour along Lake Garda's shore: villas not visible from the roadside are revealed in all their splendour, and the yellow fruits are a beautiful feature of the old lemon groves. An ideal starting point for these sightseeing tours on the water is Gargnano.

What about the food? The food is excellent everywhere. That applies regardless of whether you opt for pizza, pasta, risotto or a polenta dish, order a lavish three-course meal in a gourmet restaurant in Salò, or plump for a simple grilled Lake Garda trout. It also goes for the wine. Whether your taste is fruity and light or dry and spicy, Lake Garda is a wine-growing area suitable for different wine varieties. In the north, the red, full-bodied Marzemino goes well with hearty fare, while in the south a well-chilled rosé Bardolino Chiaretto perfectly complements fish dishes.

Nowadays, life on the lake is largely governed by tourism. Unfortunately, this is a mixed blessing for the region. The heavy traffic, in particular, is a problem. A good tip when holidaying on the lake is to avoid using a car as much as possible! On the positive side, Italians appreciate tourists, and you will be warmly welcomed, as if you have been a regular visitor for years. Happy holidays!

AT A GLANCE

24 million
annual overnight stays

London: 125.2 million

346m

Greatest depth of the lake

158km
coastline

Lake Windermere: 42km

370km²
area (largest lake in Italy)

Lake Windermere: 14.7km²

SHORTEST TRIBUTARY

175m

River Aril in Cassone

COLDEST WATER TEMPERATURE

6°C

HIGHEST PEAK

2,218m

Monte Baldo

5 ISLANDS IN THE LAKE

Isola del Garda, Isola di San Biagio, Isola del Trimelone, Isola dell'Olivo, Isola del Sogno

DESENZANO

Biggest town on the lake with approx. 30,000 inhabitants

A FISH THAT ONLY OCCURS IN LAKE GARDA

Carpione

(Lake Garda trout)

UNDERSTAND LAKE GARDA

ICY DIP & TRADITION

Have you ever been cold? *Ice*-cold? No? Then, visit Riva del Garda on New Year's Day. Plenty of people living close to Lake Garda welcome in the new year with a proverbial dip in the ice-chilled water. For the past 20 years, on New Year's Day from 11am about 100 daredevil swimmers arrive to take to the water in temperatures around zero and join in the *Tuffo di Capodanno*. Clad in bathing suits, everybody waits for the starting signal on the main piazza before swimming once around the harbour. All age groups join in – from ten-year-olds to healthy retirees. You can watch the event on *short. travel/gar22*. In Pieve, at nearby Lake Ledro, they wait until the end of the month, which, according to legend, is when the three coldest days of the year occur – the so-called *giorni della merla*, or "days of the merla (blackbird hen)". Since 2008, about 80 partici-pants take the plunge into the icy waters of Lake Ledro, traditionally known as the *Tuffo della Merla*.

WHATSAPP UPDATES FROM FISHERMEN

When Alberto Rania arrives at Piazza Battisti in Riva around 10am, the locals are already standing in a queue. They are all waiting for him to open his three-wheeler "Ape", which has been converted into a refrigerated transporter, to reveal the shiny fish on ice. About 40 different fish varieties live in Lake Garda. There are many local varieties as well as several that have accidentally arrived in the lake from the surrounding rivers, and others that were deliberately introduced. Alberto worked in a paper factory for 25 years until, in 2015, he decided on a career change. Now he is among the last 50 professional fishermen on Lake Garda. Most of them have joined cooperatives that manage the sale and processing of the fish. At the Cooperativa Pescatori in Garda, for example, the day's fresh catch is auctioned. But Alberto is self-employed and sells the day's fresh fish every Tuesday and Friday from 10am to noon in front of the castle in Riva. Regular customers receive WhatsApp updates about the day's catch. The fish are then cleaned and set aside. Anyone who is interested can also receive helpful cooking tips at *alberto rania.it*.

TUNNELS & AMAZING PANORAMIC VIEWS

Expletives can be heard from many a car driver: there are 74 tunnels along the 30km stretch of road from Riva del Garda to Gargnano. Some are so narrow that two motorhomes can only just pass, and if there is a group of cyclists then… However, the Gardesana Occidentale is considered one of the most beautiful roads in Italy. And wherever openings in tunnels and galleries reveal glimpses of the lake, then you'll realise why. It was built after World War I, not for tourists, but to link the north of the lake – which at that time became part of Italy – to the south. The slightly wider and not quite so spectacular Gardesana Orientale runs along the opposite shore. Because the old roads cannot cope with today's volume of traffic, both routes are closed to lorries in the summer.

WINTER ON THE LAKE

Admit it, you've never thought of spending winter on Lake Garda. That's a mistake! Winter is the most relaxed season and the time when locals take their bikes out of the cellar and parking meters are covered in plastic sheeting. Of course, not all the shops and bars are open and many of the hotels are shut – but that's more than made up for by the peace and quiet

everywhere. The best thing is the weather. Unlike in summer, the mist rarely descends, but the days are clear and the sky is blue. Then there's the deep blue water of the lake, the green palms and olive trees and the white mountain summits in the north. If you are protected from the wind, you can remove your sweater and enjoy the sunshine. What's more, there is a wide variety of winter sports! Theoretically, you can enjoy skiing on Monte Stivo one day and go ice climbing the next day, while on the third day you can climb in Massone – in a T-shirt, if you are lucky. There is even a small skiing area on Monte Baldo. The real surprise is the Christmas season: Christmas markets have recently become popular, especially with the residents. In Riva, Bardolino, Garda or Tremosine

Grand scenery but prone to traffic jams: the Gardesana Occidentale

– the Christmas lights twinkle every-where and seasonal treats, toys and handcrafted souvenirs are available to purchase at the wooden stalls. Many of the markets are open until early January.

NAKED OR NOT NAKED

Sauna culture in northern and south-ern climates tends to vary, especially when it's a question of whether to go naked or not. It's no different on Lake Garda. Older generations of Italians wouldn't dream of going naked in public. Meanwhile, more and more public saunas display signs suggest-ing that it is healthier not to wear bathing costumes in the sauna. This is not to say that Italians will have a change of heart.

FLAVOURSOME GOLDEN THREADS

Lake Garda is well known as the source of many special culinary ingredients, especially olive oil and wine. However, a little-known fact is that it is also the source of a legendary spice: saffron, a variety of crocus with fragrant threads grows around the lake. The locals use the precious spice not only to flavour their *risotto alla milanese*, but also to season numerous regional speciali-ties such as the crust on the Alpine cheese *tombea* and the crunchy *torta sbrisolona*, the traditional tart from the southern end of Lake Garda. In some places, even mashed potato is coloured golden yellow. The saffron is mainly cultivated at the foot of Monte Baldo, in Pravelle, Gargnano and Val

During the Christmas period, Lake Garda is romantic and there are no crowds

di Ledro. Saffron is easily confused with the poisonous large purple crocus *(Crocus speciosus)* so it is not advisable to pick your own! In Pozzolengo, at the *Azienda Agricola Al Muràs (zafferanodi pozzolengo.it)* fine quality organic saffron has been successfully cultivated – about 3kg a year. In other words, approximately 600,000 saffron flowers are harvested by hand and a part of them is immediately processed into fine delicacies. You can try some at the farm's store!

INSIDER TIP
Golden spice from Lake Garda

TREASURE FROM MONTE BALDO

The truffle (or *tartufo* in Italian) is a fungus – but what a misnomer for

TRUE OR FALSE?

LAKE GARDA IS ITALIAN

German poet Goethe is partly to blame for our understanding of Lake Garda as a Mediterranean holiday destination, because – in his *Italian Journey* – he talked of figs and olives. Indeed, oranges and lemons do grow around Lake Garda, and people do eat pizza and *gelato*; but the northern part of the lake was under Austrian Habsburg rule for a long time, and they left behind their culinary heritage, such as *canederli*, or dumplings, which come in all sorts, including bacon.

such an exquisite culinary delight! They grow underground among the roots of deciduous trees. Regions in this guide known for their truffles are Monte Baldo on the eastern shore and Parco Alto Garda Bresciano on the western side of Lake Garda. In autumn, Tignale hosts the truffle festival *Sagra del Tartufo (tignale.org)*. Pigs were traditionally used to snuffle out truffles which they reliably found – but were only too eager to gobble up themselves. Nowadays dogs are used instead. Hunting for truffles in restricted by law: only official *tartufari* are allowed to dig for the expensive mushrooms. Private individuals looking for truffles can be fined for poaching!

CITRIC YOUTH

Alberto Dagnoli is proud of the fact that he is over 70 years old and healthy. His secret: plenty of fresh fish, olive oil and of course lemons. The pensioner is a tourist guide and is passionate about accompanying all those who are interested through the lemon groves in Limone. He knows the inhabitants of Limone live longer – his own grandparents were working well into their old age. In fact, the reason the *Limonesi* enjoy particularly long lives has less to do with the diet of the residents of this once-isolated fishing village. Instead, it is because of a genetic mutation that helps to concentrate cholesterol in the blood and to transport it to the liver, so preventing cardiovascular disease. It affects about 40 residents in the village and Alberto's brother – unlike

Alberto – is one of the lucky ones. Never mind, Alberto feels fit and healthy, and he swears by his daily intake of sour citrus fruits!

OIL FOR CONNOISSEURS

Lake Garda without olive oil? That would be like Munich without the beer! Ivo Bertamini laughs. He is an olive-grower in the north of Lake Garda and, for about the last 50 years, he has managed a traditional olive oil press or *frantoio* near Arco *(www. gardatrentino.it/en/info/frantoio-bertamini_3905)*. "We press the olives with a real millstone. Compared with the oils from industrial high-tech mills, our oil tastes softer and less spicy." For several years, he has also been producing cosmetic products like soap, shampoo and creams. However, it's not all about large-scale production. Many families have a few trees on the terraces and gardens around the lake and produce their own oil. This is labour-intensive work. Not many people who dress their salad with olive oil from Lake Garda realize that all the olives here are harvested by hand. One tree yields about 20–30kg. Two experienced pickers can harvest a maximum of 100kg of olives in a day, which makes about 15–18 litres of oil. It's hardly surprising that one litre of high-quality olive oil can easily cost 25 or 30 euros.

INSIDER TIP
Natural skincare

HISTORY ON THE LAKEBED

Divers' hearts beat faster in 2017 when a relic of seafaring history was

Hard work: olive farmers will tell you why oil sold for 5 euros per litre can't be great quality

discovered in Lake Garda. The wreck of a cargo ship was located about 150m deep and halfway between Maderno on the western shore and Torri del Benaco on the eastern shore. The accident must have occurred in the 17th century. Those who are interested can look at the photos on Facebook by visiting "La storia sommersa – Lago di Garda".

HIS MAJESTY THE CODFISH

It's normal for architectural monuments, famous people, animals and plants to feature on postage stamps.

But food? In 2017, for the first time in the history of philately, this honour was granted to a recipe for dried cod, the *baccalà alla vicentina* from the area to the southeast of Lake Garda. The 0.95-euro stamp features the terracotta pot used to cook this speciality from Vicenza, a few pieces of dried cod and a bowl of polenta. Visit *baccalaallavicentina.it* to read (in Italian) about how the Norwegian cod became a classic dish in Vicenza.

EATING
SHOPPING
SPORT

Olive oil and grappa, cheese and wine: tempting *Delicatezze del Garda*

ALIMENTARI
DA LINA
LICATEZZE DEL GARDA

CORSO
GARIBALDI

5

EATING & DRINKING

Food in the Lake Garda region, as in the rest of Italy, is more than just nourishment: food is culture. As the lake borders the three regions of Trentino, Lombardy and Veneto, there is no Lake Garda cuisine per se. However, the sheer variety of regional specialities found in kitchens around the lake makes for an intriguing culinary excursion.

The common denominator for all three regions is the fact that they draw on Alpine traditions as well as their proximity to the water. And, of course, you can choose from a large selection of good (fish) restaurants.

DELICACIES FROM THE LAKE

The gastronomic palette around the lake includes excellent freshwater fish such as trout *(trota)*, Lake Garda whitefish *(coregone)*, vendace *(lavarello)*, pike *(luccio)* and perch *(persico)*. There is also the Lake Garda trout *(carpione*

del Garda), although you might want to abstain from this dish because the species is threatened with extinction. If you discover *sardine di lago* on the menu, you should grab the opportunity. It is really quite rare. Sardines are normally found in the sea, but there is one sub-species of the herring family, called twaite shad in English, that lives in Lake Garda. The sardines are cut into small pieces and mixed with pasta. *Spaghetti con sardine di lago* is still a much-loved delicacy today.

ALPINE CUISINE

The cuisine in northern Trentino is quite substantial. You will often come across hearty dishes such as polenta with rabbit *(coniglio)*, *strangolapreti* (spinach gnocchi, delicious with butter and sage) or *canederli* (dumplings) on the menu. Some of these dishes are almost too heavy for a summer evening by the lake. They are just a

Soul food from Lake Garda: polenta with bacon and chanterelles (left); grilled fish (right)

reminder that maybe one should try visiting Lake Garda in winter. Another benefit of a winter stay is that December is the truffle-picking season on the slopes of Monte Baldo. Truffles *(tartufi)* are a natural delicacy. You should definitely try *carne salada*, which is a kind of cured meat that is a true Trentino speciality. It is either served raw like carpaccio as a starter or stewed with beans and onions. Tagliatelle with mushrooms or *risotto ai funghi porcini* also bring an Alpine flair to the table.

RISOTTI & TORTELLINI

On the eastern side of the lake bordering the Veneto, polenta is also a popular food. However, it is usually finer in texture and creamy rather than firm because it is made of husked kernels from a lighter coloured corn. Although trade has always flourished in the Veneto and its people have become familiar with foods from Asia and Africa, the local cuisine is still simple and largely influenced by the north. Beans, fish and offal often come into play. As sprawling rice fields can be found to the south of Verona in the Po valley, there are all sorts of risotti on menus. When it comes to pasta, the locals prefer thick spaghetti called *bigoli*. Although the hand-made *tortellini di Valeggio* from the town of the same name south of Peschiera are no longer an insider tip, they are still unbelievably delicious.

UNUSUAL MEATS

Lombardy has the largest stretch of the shoreline, running from Limone in the north on the western shore past Salò and south to Sirmione. The locals in this area love hearty soups, savoury stewed meat or a *spiedo* (skewer) of different kinds of meats with bacon in between that is grilled over an open fire. Of course, you will also find plenty of polenta in Lombardy! If your taste buds are yearning for something more adventurous, look for horse meat, frog's legs or snails on the menu.

SALUTE!

The choice of drinks around the lake is alsovery diverse. The hearty food of the north calls for full-blooded wines: two delicious red wines exclusively pressed in the Trentino are Teroldego and Marzemino. The north is also famous for its grappas. This fragrant, grape-based pomace liquor is normally drunk "neat", sometimes flavoured with pine needles, rowan berries or gentian root. Some distilleries store their grappa in wooden casks so that the liquor takes on its golden colour

INSIDER TIP
Golden grappa

and looks like whisky. The excellent *vino santo* from the area around Lake Toblino is less well known. Made from nosiola grapes that are dried on wooden slats by the winds of Lake Garda, this dessert wine is pressed in the *settimana santa* (Holy Week).

On the eastern shore, the typical wine is red Bardolino. Once discredited as a "mass-produced wine", it is now of good quality. If you want to learn more about it, drive down the Strada del Vino. Fine white wines such as the Lugana, in particular, are found in the southeast. As an aperitif or an after-meal drink, keep an eye out for the sparkling wines from Franciacorta in the southwest, made using the *méthode champenoise*.

BIRRA ALLA LAGO

An Aperol Spritz or a glass of wine – that's all part of a holiday on the lake. However, young Italians increasingly order craft beer produced by microbreweries from the southern area of the lake or unfiltered beer from the Ledro Valley. Beer comes *alla spina* (from the cask) or *in bottiglia* (in the bottle).

A final tip: supermarkets or delicatessens sell many regional specialties at reasonable prices: local cheese and salami, olives and pickled vegetables, fresh bread – and of course tomatoes, mozzarella and basil. Find a nice spot on the beach, on a jetty or a mountain slope and enjoy a picnic al fresco. *Buon appetito!*

Bardolino is produced on the eastern shore

TODAY'S SPECIALS

Antipasti

SARDE IN SAÒR
Marinated fried sardines with caramelised onions, pine nuts and raisins

CARNE SALADA
Beef rump, flavoured and spiced, thinly cut and served raw

FIORI DI ZUCCA RIPIENI
Stuffed courgette flowers (usually filled with ricotta)

Primi piatti

BIGOLI CON LE SARDE
Thick spaghetti with anchovies

RISOTTO CON LE TINCHE
Risotto with Lake Garda tench

TORTELLINI DI ZUCCA
Ravioli stuffed with pumpkin

STRANGOLAPRETI BURRO E SALVIA
Spinach dumplings with butter and sage

Secondi Piatti

TROTA IN SAÒR
Trout marinated with onions and white wine

LUCCIO IN SALSA
Pike in a sauce made from fried sardines

ALBORELLE
Fried lake fish

LAVARELLO ALLA GRIGLIA
Grilled Lake Garda vendace

COTOLETTA ALLA MILANESE
Milan-style breaded cutlets

BOLLITO MISTO
Stew with boiled chicken, veal and beef, served with a pickled sauce

FARAONA RIPIENA
Stuffed guinea fowl

PASTISSADA DE CAVAL
Horse-meat stew, slow-cooked in red wine

Dolci

MACEDONIA
Fresh fruit salad

TORTA SBRISOLONA
A strudel-likel cake that is served broken into pieces, not sliced

SHOPPING

LAKE GARDA DELICACIES

Local delicacies make particularly suitable presents, and the trick is to know what to buy best and where. The best (and cheapest) place to buy the wonderfully mild Lake Garda olive oil is at a cooperative, for example in Riva, Gargnano or Limone. You should buy cheese in a *caseificio* (dairy), such as in San Zeno di Montagna or Tremosine. Wine and grappa are best bought either at the vineries along the Strada del Vino or else in supermarkets or from specialist wine retailers. Beware, in souvenir shops the packaging may be pretty and appealing to tourists, but the contents may not necessarily be the best. If you like *prosciutto* and mortadella, here's a tip: many supermarkets will shrink-wrap the meats for you so that they will last the journey home.

INSIDER TIP
Take it home shrink-wrapped

STRAIGHT FROM THE CATWALK

Leather goods are still reasonably priced in Italy, especially at markets. Italian designer fashion is available in the brand boutiques of Salò and Peschiera, Desenzano, Riva and Bardolino. You can often find bargains if you're there in late summer. In end-of-season sales *(saldi)*, many shops discount their goods by 50 per cent. The savings are particularly worthwhile with genuine designer clothes. Just watch out for super-cheap ware because it might be a forgery or of low quality.

A PARADISE FOR SPORTSPEOPLE

With so many sporting types in the Lake Garda area, there is no shortage of suitable sports shops. In Torbole, windsurfers can buy everything they need for their sport, from flashy boards and state-of-the-art equipment to waterproof clothing. Climbers and

Take the aroma and taste of the region home by buying soap (left) and olive oil (right)

mountaineers are catered for (among other places) in Arco, where you can sometimes get cheap mountain gear, while mountain bikers can get spare parts especially in Torbole or Arco.

BELLA ITALIA FOR YOUR FRONT DOOR

Would you like to greet visitors at the door with a touch of the Mediterranean? Attractive house number signs are on sale everywhere in Limone. Made from ceramics and decorated with lemons, they are bound to lift the mood!

FACTORY OUTLET BARGAINS

Outlet shopping is becoming more popular, especially south of the lake. You can find bargain deals on brand-named goods, for example, directly at *Bialetti*, a speciality manufacturer of coffee and kitchen equipment. Their factory outlet is located in *Coccaglio*, 25km west of Brescia *(Via Fogliano 1)*, and offers Bialetti products with a 10–20 per cent discount. Underwear, hosiery and bikinis are for sale in Avio (Ala-Avio exit from the A22) at the *Calzedonia Intimissimi Outlet (Via del Lavoro 30/at the corner of Via dei Carri).*

FOR HAIR & SKIN

Several shops, mainly on the eastern and southern shore, sell cosmetics produced from oil, lemons or grapes from Lake Garda. We recommend, for example, *Vita Lake (Borgo Garibaldi 19 | vitalake.com)* in Bardolino. Their body cream is made with lemons from the Riviera dei Limoni and the body scrub contains red wine from Bardolino. All very tempting!

SPORT & ACTIVITIES

Lake Garda is known and loved for its sports. For decades, the winds have drawn windsurfers and sailors onto the water. Climbers and mountain bikers cherish the limestone walls and steep trails in the north. Even if you only want to hike, bathe and go boating, this adult adventure playground is a great place for your holiday.

CANYONING

It is not possible to take part in some adventure sports without professional instruction. Canyoning is one of them. The following organisers provide guided tours: *XMountain (Via Frà Giovanni da Schio 1e | San Giovanni Lupatoto | tel. 34 81 46 37 00 | xmountain.it); Canyon Adventures (Via Matteotti 122 | Torbole | tel. 33 48 69 86 66 | canyonadv.com); Mmove (Via Legionari Cecolsovacci 14 | Arco | tel. 33 81 93 33 74 | mmove.net);* *Skyclimber (Via Provinciale 1 | Tremosine | tel. 34 81 99 71 99 | skyclimber.it)*

CLIMBING & BOULDERING

Apparently, the cradle of European climbing sports is in Arco. It's true that there are over 2,000 climbing routes that cater for practically every level of difficulty, and there are more climbing outfitters than supermarkets. Those who prefer not to climb solo can join the local mountain guides – ranging from a fun climb to climbing for children and all types of courses. When the weather is stormy or it rains, there is an indoor alternative in the Sarca Valley: *Campfour Boulder (opening times are weather dependent, visit FB for updates, mostly Tue 3–11pm, Wed–Fri 11am–10pm, Sat/Sun 11am–8pm | Viale Daino 74 |*

INSIDER TIP
Raining? I don't mind!

The northern shore is a climber's paradise: rocks along the Via dell'Amicizia above Riva

Pietramurata | campfourboulder.it). Rock Master (rockmaster.com), the climbing competition held in late summer in Arco, attracts the world's free-climbing elite and is a spectacular experience for onlookers.

CYCLING & MOUNTAIN BIKING

The north is the most popular area for ambitious cyclists. The *Mountain & Garda Bike* trail *(mountaingardabike. com)* stretches over 218km and climbs a total of 10,000m. The *Bike Festival (riva.bike-festival.de/en)* is held around Riva in late April/early May.

⚑ Monte Baldo is the most popular destination for fit mountain bikers. Those who want to avoid the grind of uphill riding can take the cable car from Malcesine, which also transports bikes at certain times. Not only can you hire bikes from *Xtreme* at the cable car station in the valley *(Via* Navene Vecchia 10 | tel. 04 57 40 01 05 | xtrememalcesine.com), but they will even transport them to the top of Monte Baldo.

The province of Verona has introduced the *Bus & Bike service (tel. 04 58 05 79 22 | atv.verona.it/Walk_e_ Bike)* for the summer months: you take the scheduled bus service, which also transports bikes, from Garda up to San Zeno di Montagna or Prada on the slopes of Monte Baldo, and from there it is downhill all the way.

If you're looking for a more relaxed way to explore the lake on a bike, try the different trails through the countryside along the shore. Although it is still not possible to cycle around the entire lake, new stretches of the trail are opening every year.

DIVING

Diving centres offering courses and tours can be found, among others, in

Torri del Benaco, Riva, Salò and Desenzano. *Arco Sub (tel. 34 00 04 56 51 | arcosub.com)* in Torbole runs courses.

HIKING

You've just walked past a castle, paused to rest beneath an olive tree – and now you are standing between rugged rock formations before heading across expansive mountain meadows: these contrasts account for the charm of hiking along Lake Garda. The most beautiful areas are Monte Baldo, the Alto Garda Bresciano nature park on the western shore, the Ledro Valley and Lake Tenno in the north and Rocca di Garda, the Mincio Valley and Rocca di Manerba in the south.

The *Sentiero della Pace* is worth seeing. It extends for over 500km from the Stelvio Pass as far as Marmolada along the World War I frontline. It links ramparts and fortress sites, tunnels and cemeteries as well as large and small museums. The southern leg between Riva and Rovereto *(short. travel/gar20)* with Monte Brione is easily accessible. The impressions of the countryside along this hiking trail are often spectacular. However, thoughtful hikers will be reminded at every step of the terrible events that occurred along the route. An estimate of the victims who fell in the mountains during the war between 1915 and 1918 is up to 150,000 or 180,000 soldiers on both sides.

JOGGING & TRAIL RUNNING

Are you a keen jogger? Don't forget your running shoes, as the lakeside promenades, pebbly routes, paths and trails around the lake are a paradise for joggers. Those with a competitive streak can choose from the following options: *Lake Garda Marathon (lakegardamarathon.com)*, skyrunning in the *Limone Extreme Skyrace (limonextreme.com)* or the *Garda Trentino Half Marathon (trentino eventi.it)*.

RIDING

Riding and horseback tours are organised by *Ranch Il Bosco (Puegnago sul Garda | tel. 03 65 55 55 05 | ranchilbosco.it); Scuderia Castello (Toscolano-Maderno | tel. 03 65 64 41 01 | scuderiacastello.it); Club Ippico San Giorgio (Arco | tel. 34 84 43 83 07 | clubippicosangiorgio.it).*

SAILING

Since the 1960s, Lake Garda has been one of Europe's most popular sailing locations thanks to its constant winds. There are sailing schools everywhere on the lake. Every year almost 100 regattas are held, the most famous being the *Centomiglia (centomiglia.it)* in September in Bogliaco.

WINDSURFING & KITESURFING

The supreme discipline on Lake Garda, which is particularly well suited for windsurfing because its northern section emerges from a narrow mountain valley through which regular winds blow as if from a jet. Torbole on the northern shore is the surfers' mecca, while in Riva conditions are also suitable for beginners. One more advantage of the north is that motorboats are not permitted in the Trentino section of the lake. In addition to Torbole, the surfing schools renting boards are mainly concentrated in Riva, Malcesine and Gargnano. Kitesurfing is quickly gaining in popularity. Most surf schools have included this trendy sport in their portfolio. Stand-up paddleboarding is now also fashionable on Lake Garda, with many surf schools running courses and renting boards for you to paddle at your leisure. However, it is advisable to get accustomed to the winds beforehand and choose a quieter time so that the fun doesn't suddenly turn into a stressful event.

YOGA

Have you tried meditating on a stand-up paddleboard? Or greeted the rising sun and practised yoga on a mountain meadow? At Lake Garda, yogis have countless opportunities to calm their mind and balance their body while on holiday.

On the northern shore, yoga teacher *Giulia Bazzanella (mindfulyogabird. wixsite.com/yoga)* in Arco offers individual sessions on the beach in Riva or at Arco castle. In the south, *Indigo-Yoga (indigoyoga.eu)* in Desenzano run yoga lessons on a stand-up paddleboard. On the eastern shore, teachers Annette Füchsle-Reiter and Renate Gronbach run yoga weeks for beginners and advanced students in their *Yogarda studio (yogarda.de)* in San Zeno di Montagna. The *Sagar Yoga (sagar. yoga/it)* school in Toscolano-Maderno on the western shore allows you to choose between various courses, including family yoga.

There is no question that windsurfing is the number one sport on Lake Garda

REGIONAL OVERVIEW

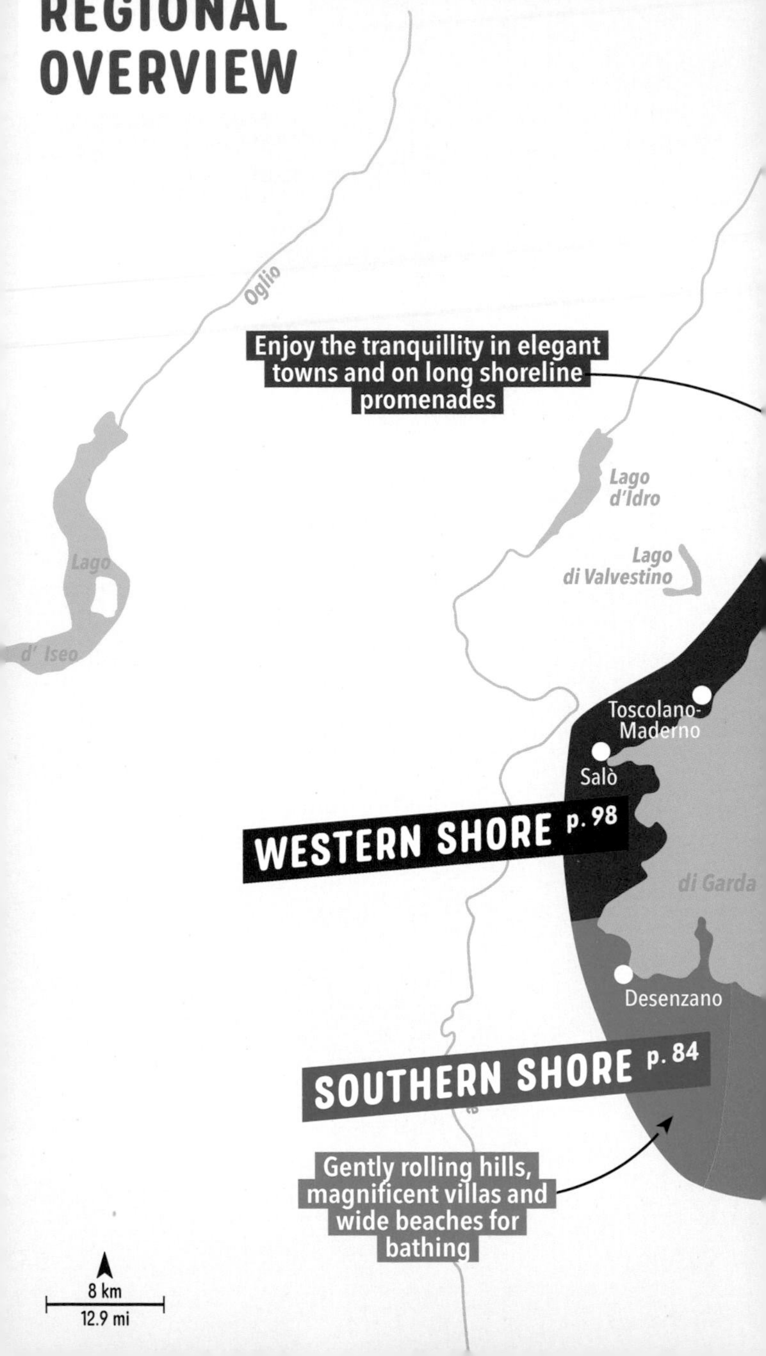

Oglio

Lago d'Idro

Lago di Valvestino

Lago d' Iseo

Enjoy the tranquillity in elegant towns and on long shoreline promenades

Toscolano-Maderno

Salò

WESTERN SHORE p. 98

di Garda

Desenzano

SOUTHERN SHORE p. 84

Gently rolling hills, magnificent villas and wide beaches for bathing

8 km
12.9 mi

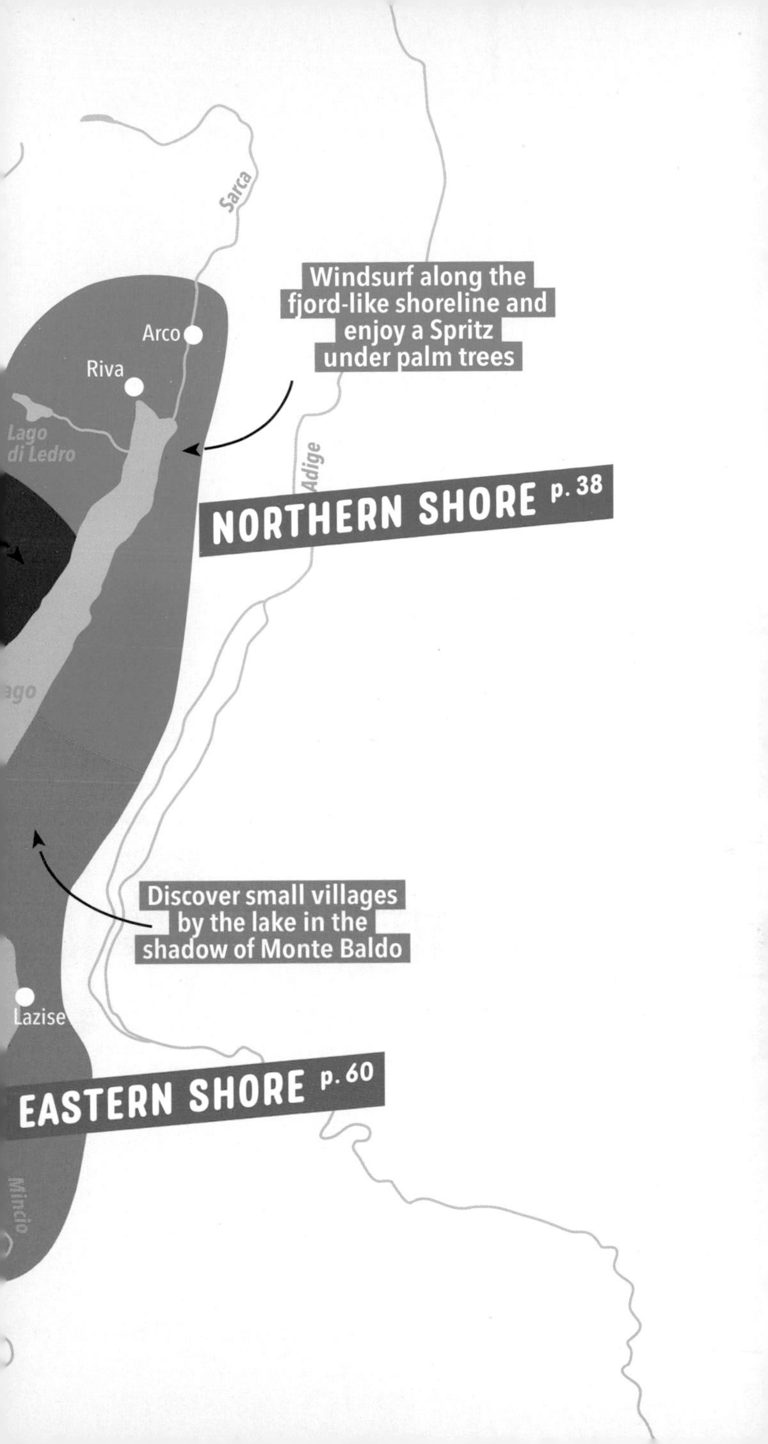

Sarca

Arco

Riva

Lago
di Ledro

**Windsurf along the
fjord-like shoreline and
enjoy a Spritz
under palm trees**

Adige

NORTHERN SHORE p. 38

ago

**Discover small villages
by the lake in the
shadow of Monte Baldo**

Lazise

EASTERN SHORE p. 60

Mincio

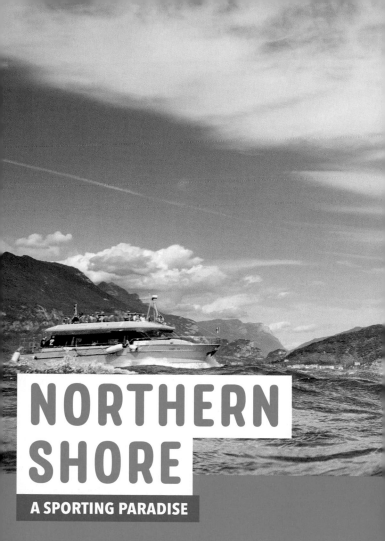

NORTHERN SHORE

A SPORTING PARADISE

You can skip that trip to a distant Norwegian fjord. Instead, go to the north end of Lake Garda, which has the same spectacular scenery. The sheer mountain faces leave little room for settlements, but down below is where olive and palm trees grow.

Riva del Garda is the only place with room for expansion. The neighbouring village of Torbole is hemmed in between Monte Brione, the lake shore and the bluff on which the ruins of Penede castle are perched. This location is what visitors most value about Torbole – it

The constant wind draws windsurfers to the northern shore

creates a wind channel through which the *ora*, *pelér* and *balì* winds regularly blow, much to the enjoyment of the surfing community.

Further south you come to the pretty little village of Malcesine which, unfortunately, is often overcrowded. Keen climbers ascend the almost 2,000-m-high peak of Monte Baldo that towers over the lake. Directly opposite, Limone, with its lemon greenhouses, sometimes seems to groan under the throng of day trippers. The charm of this small place is best savoured early in the morning.

NORTHERN SHORE

Breguzzo
Bondo
Roncone
Daone
Bersone
Creto
Cologna
Castel Condino
237
Cimego
Lenzumo
Camp
Tiarno di Sotto
Bezzecca
Locca
Condino
240
Tiarno di Sopra
Pieve di Ledro
Mezzolago
3 Lago di Ledro
Bia
di L
Molina di Ledro
Ca' Rossa
LOMBARDIA
Storo
Lago di Tenno
14 km, 20 min
P

Limone sul Garda
p. 42

MARCO POLO HIGHLIGHTS

★ **RIVA DEL GARDA**
Stroll through the town centre, enjoying a gelato. For over 100 years, visitors, including many writers, have been seduced by the charm of the mainly traffic-free town on the northern shore ➤ p. 44

★ **CASTELLO DI ARCO**
This castle high above the small town has views of olive groves; it also has a frightening dungeon ➤ p. 54

★ **CASTELLO SCALIGERO**
Even German poet Goethe was spellbound by the beauty of this old Scaliger castle by the lake ➤ p. 55

★ **FUNIVIA MALCESINE–MONTE BALDO**
Enjoy far-reaching views from the cable car and the summit ➤ p. 57

Pieve
45
Spiaggia Paina
Funivia Malcesine–Monte Baldo ★
Malcesine
p. 54
Campione del Garda
Castello Scaligero ★
Tignale
Cassone **11**
Eremo Santi Benigno e Caro **10**
Assenza
Muslone
di Garda
Porto
Magugnano
11 Brenzone

Come by boat – Limone looks best from the water!

LIMONE SUL GARDA

(□ H–J3) **In this village on the northwestern shore, lemons are grown in greenhouses on the mountain slopes, and many shops sell T-shirts, bags or kitchenware that are decorated with the citrus fruit. Limone? Most people think that the name of the place comes from the lemon, when in fact it is derived from the Latin term *limes*, pointing to the former border between Austria and Italy, which once ran through the village.**

Nevertheless, lemons have determined the life of the people here for centuries. When some monks in the Middle Ages brought the exotic fruits to Lake Garda, the Limonesi provided them with perfect growing conditions around their remote fishing village. In 1750, the first fruits could be harvested, but these were not intended for the locals. Instead, they served as precious goods for bartering and quickly became coveted merchandise.

Lake Garda still guarantees a particularly mild microclimate year-round. Nevertheless, the peak tourist season is restricted to the summer months and from November Limone quietens down for the winter. Many shops, restaurants and hotels close, parking meters are wrapped in plastic and car park barriers are dismantled. Now, the village is solely for the enjoyment of its approximately 1,000 residents. Today, lemons are still used in many dishes and cakes or are sliced thinly and eaten with brown sugar or drunk chilled as Limoncello. However, these days the town's focus is more on tourism than on lemon cultivation.

SIGHTSEEING

MUSEO DEL TURISMO 🐷

The local community has taken great care to collect old photos, newspaper articles and much more about the (tourism) history of the village. The small museum is in the centre of the Old Town and opens until late. Admission is free. *April and Oct daily 10am–6pm, May–Sept 10am–10pm | Via Monsignor Daniele Comboni 3*

LIMONAIA DEL CASTEL

Smell the fine scent of almost 50 citrus tree species in this renovated 18th-century conservatory. The *limonaia* is also an open-air museum. *Easter–mid Sept daily 10am–10pm, mid-Sept–Oct 10am–6pm | Via Orti 9 | ⏲ 1 hr*

PARCO VILLA BOGHI

Had enough of the crowds in the narrow lanes of the Old Town? Then relax in the manicured gardens of Villa Boghi. Here, there is also a small fishing museum and an old-fashioned *limonaia*, a conservatory for cultivating lemons. *Daily 8am–10pm | Via IV Novembre 42*

EATING & DRINKING

HOTEL AL RIO SÈ

Regulars have been returning to this small hotel somewhat off the beaten track for decades. It's very quiet on the terrace of the restaurant where you can enjoy a wonderful fillet of trout with fresh sage and butter. *Open daily April–Oct | Via Nova 12 | tel. 03 65 95 41 82 | alriose.com | €*

SPAGHETTIHAUS

High above the lake you can sit on the extensive terrace or in the garden with a pool and choose between eight different spaghetti dishes. In addition, there are fabulous views of Monte Baldo at sunset. Fair prices, a lounge atmosphere and delicious food! *Daily | Via Prealzo 4a | tel. 03 65 95 46 35 | €–€€*

INSIDER TIP
Pasta with a view

SHOPPING

COOPERATIVA AGRICOLA POSSIDENTI OLIVETI

The shop of this "cooperative of olive grove owners" sells *olio d'oliva extra vergine* as well as other related products such as olives and paste. All olives are grown locally. *Via Campaldo 10 and Via IV Novembre 29 | oleificio limonesulgarda.it*

FRUTTO DEL GARDA

Fans of citrus fruits should visit this small organic farm (phone beforehand). The Risatti couple have lovingly planted about 150 trees (by hand) and use the fruits to make jams, liqueurs and syrups. *Via Campaldo 12 | tel. 34 01 08 50 19 | fruttodelgarda.it*

MARKET

From Easter to October there is a market in the town centre every Tuesday from 8am to 3pm.

SPORT & ACTIVITIES

CYCLING

In 2018, the first leg of the Lake Garda bike path was opened between Limone and Capo Reamol, a few kilometres to the north. The "Garda by Bike" project intends to construct a 140-km circular path around the entire lake. It will, in parts, run through tunnels while in other places a steel construction along the mountain slope is planned. Whereas some have called it the "world's most beautiful cycle trail", environmentalists fear that an excessive number of trees will have to be felled for its construction.

HIKING

From May to October, the tourist association organises 🐷 free guided hikes, for example to the Bonaventura Segala mountain refuge. For information, please talk to the tourist information office and visit *visit limonesulgarda.com*.

SAILING & WINDSURFING

Surfing Lino (tel. 33 84 09 74 90 | surfinglino.com) at the Spiaggia Fonte Torrente San Giovanni offer cat sailing and windsurfing courses.

BEACHES

Access to the beaches in Limone is free of charge, although most car parks nearby charge a fee. The wide pebble beach of *Spiaggia Cola* stretches along the promenade, and you can play beach volleyball on the adjacent *Spiaggia Fonte Torrente San Giovanni*.

WELLNESS

If you book in advance, the *Hotel du Lac* offers non-residents access to its *spa (Mon–Sat 9am–7pm | 20 euros | Via Fasse 1 | tel. 03 65 95 44 81 | dulac-limone.it)*, which has a whirlpool, sauna and Turkish bath.

NIGHTLIFE

Nightlife is not the priority in Limone. After dinner, you can stroll through the streets of the old town centre where you will have no trouble finding somewhere to drink a Spritz. In summer, there are also concerts.

RIVA DEL GARDA

(▥ J2) **Big city life, just on a smaller scale:** ★ **Riva (pop. 16,000) is the most urban among the towns on the northern shore.**

Local people, who still outnumber the many tourists even in summer, enjoy fashion and good clothes, the restaurants are chic and shopping focuses on boutiques and shoe shops rather than climbing and cycling outfitters. While other towns on the northern shore are deserted in winter, Riva is lit throughout the year: when the lights of the summer festivals have extinguished, residents switch on the Christmas decorations.

How did this evolve? In the 19th century when the town was still

Charming Riva has had a cosmopolitan vibe since the 19th century

governed by Austria-Hungary, Riva, which was already popular, became a busy spa town. First, it was only visited by the Habsburgs; later American millionaires arrived as well as Russian aristocrats. They were attracted by the mild climate, culture and numerous places for excursions. Not much has changed today. The town and its lively pedestrian zone, many shops and narrow alleys is a popular resort all year round – for families as well as holidaymakers with an interest in all kinds of sports. Enjoy this wonderful mixture of Italian *dolce vita* and Alpine nature-lover's paradise!

The surrounding mountains satisfy the demands of bikers and climbers. Surfers and sailors enjoy the constant winds, and water sports fans practice their art along extensive bathing beaches. In Riva, the days don't just feel shorter, they actually are: around 5pm, and in winter as early as 3pm, Monte Rocchetta casts its shadow across the Old Town. Nevertheless, Riva remains one of the most beautiful towns on Lake Garda.

SIGHTSEEING

FORTRESS & MUSEUM

What was once designed to instil fear, now looks rather romantic. In the 12th century there was a moated castle here; now colourful fishing boats float on the water and scare away the ducks. Inside the castle is the *Museo Alto Garda MAG (mid-March–May and Oct Tue–Sun, June–Sept daily 10am–6pm |*

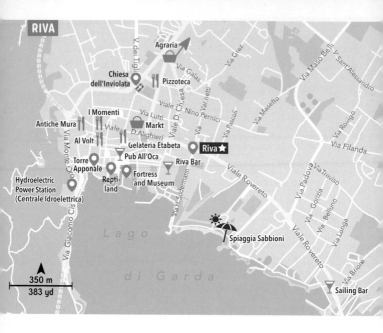

Piazza Cesare Battisti 3a | *museoalto garda.it* | (🕐 1½ hrs) which has an art gallery and exhibition on the town's history. During the 🎪 Advent season, Father Christmas even comes here: children can make their own decorations, write letters to "Babbo Natale" with their present wishes, and you can drink hot chocolate with marshmallows.

REPTILAND 🎪

This reptile house is located in the Old Town of Riva. Powerful pythons, poisonous snakes, giant spiders and scorpions await safely behind glass. Exciting for both the young and the old. *Daily 11am–8pm, reduced opening hours in Nov and Jan/Feb | 9 euros, children 8 euros, under 8s free | Piazza Garibaldi 2 | reptiland.it | 🕐 40 mins*

TORRE APPONALE

Climb the 165 steps of this tower and enjoy breathtaking views of Riva and the lake. The town's 34-m-high landmark that makes pictures of Riva so unmistakable, was built in the 13th century to protect the harbour. The busy Piazza III Novembre, the heart of the Old Town, spreads out at the foot of the tower. *March–May and Oct/Nov Tue–Sun, June–Sept daily 10am–6pm*

HYDROELECTRIC POWER STATION (CENTRALE IDROELETTRICA) 🎪

Between April and October, guided tours take you into the heart of the mountain where you will see what were at one time the biggest water turbines in the world. Interactive simulations tell the history of the power plant and how electricity is still generated here today – it's exciting and fun even for children! *Booking required: tel. 04 61 03 24 86 | 15 euros, children aged 7 and above 8 euros | Via Giacomo Cis 13 | hydrotourdolomiti.it |* ⏱ *2 hrs*

CHIESA DELL'INVIOLATA

Featuring five altars, marble floors, frescoes and stucco, this striking octagonal church was built outside the Old Town in the 17th century. It is considered the finest Baroque church in Trentino. *Viale Roma 50*

EATING & DRINKING

AL VOLT

In a *palazzo* in the town centre, the Poli family serves classics of northern Italian cuisine with a creative touch. Highly recommended are the tortelloni with an aubergine and ricotta cream. Try and get one of the outdoor tables so that you can enjoy eating in the lane. *Closed Mon | Via Fiume 73 | tel. 04 64 55 25 70 | ristorantealvolt. com | €€–€€€*

ANTICHE MURA

Here the Mediterranean meets the Dolomites. The plates served by Neapolitan chef Gianluigi Mandico are small works of art. By the end of the evening, your bank balance will have gone down, your stomach will feel nicely full and you will be the happier for it! *Closed Wed | Via Bastione 19 | tel. 04 64 55 60 63 | antiche-mura.it | €€–€€€*

GELATERIA ETABETA

You just have to try the creamy pistachio ice cream! But in summer, it's the *granite*, finely crushed ice
INSIDER TIP
Incredible ice
creations, that are most popular. The watermelon *granita* contains real fruit. *Daily 11am–11pm | Via Disciplini 14*

I MOMENTI

Cut into pieces and served with a delicious dip – for example pesto or leek cream – the pizzas in this *Enosteria Pizzeria* may look unusual but are particularly delicious. We recommend ordering two half pizzas so that you can taste several flavours. They also serve seafood platters and a superb selection of wines. *Oct–May closed Tue, mid-June–mid-Sept closed at lunchtime | Viale Prati 4c | tel. 04 64 52 05 40 | imomenti.it | €–€€*

PIZZOTECA

Authentic pizza dough, thin and crispy and with fresh ingredients – the locals in Riva love this and enjoy dining here. Try the kamut dough variety made with an ancient type of wheat:
INSIDER TIP
Try the delicious kamut pizza
it makes the pizza even crispier. The garden is pleasant in summer. *Closed Tue in winter | Viale Baruffaldi 1 | tel. 04 64 52 04 00 | €*

SHOPPING

AGRARIA

This shop belonging to a cooperative of 300 local farmers sells all kinds of

INSIDER TIP
Become an oil baron

local products such as olive oil and pickled vegetables. You can participate in a course over two evenings and become an oil sommelier (for event information visit their website). *Located in San Nazzaro 4 | store.agririva.it*

MARKET
In summer, the market is held every second and fourth Wednesday of the month in *Viale Dante*.

SPORT & ACTIVITIES

CYCLING
Bike rental shops have both normal bicycles as well as sporty MTBs, for example at the *Garda Bike Shop (Viale Rovereto 3a | gardabikeshop.com)*. They also offer to transport your bikes for a party of at least four people.

WATER SPORTS
The *Sailing du Lac (sailingdulac.com)* sailing school is located by the lake. Here, you can do a sailing or windsurfing course or simply hire a board. Otherwise, take a stand-up board and explore the shoreline.

BEACHES

Riva has one of the largest and best public beaches on the whole lake. The popular *Spiaggia Sabbioni* is a pretty pebble beach with trees, a bar where you can enjoy an aperitif, and artificial bathing islands.

You will find one beach after the other along the shoreline to Torbole.

ENTERTAINMENT

PUB ALL'OCA
A piece of England in the heart of Riva. The "Goose" pub has been a local hangout since 1982. *Daily 6pm–2am | Via Santa Maria 15 | FB: Pub all'oca*

RIVA BAR
The cocktails and *aperitivi* here are legendary with their amazing choice of snacks, from vegetable sticks to mini-pizzas. The bar organises workshops several times a year. In the evening, you can become a whisky professional or learn all you need to know about tequila. The only drawback is that these events are held in Italian. Whether this matters when you are savouring a good gin remains to be seen … *Daily 5.30pm–2am | Largo Medaglie d'Oro 1 | rivabar.it*

SAILING BAR
By San Nicolò harbour, this is the best place for a traditional Italian Aperol Spritz and cool music or a coconut juice after a day on the beach. The view of harbour and mountains from the rooftop terrace is fantastic! *Viale Rovereto 136 | FB: Sailing Bar*

AROUND RIVA DEL GARDA

1 CASCATA DEL VARONE ☂
3km north of Riva / 12 mins by bus
What peacefully shimmers up in Lago di Tenno drops with a roar into the

valley 100m below. The walk is relatively short, but still quite impressive, loud and wet. Don't forget to bring rain gear! There are few parking spaces and many visitors, so it's best if you come in the morning. *March and Oct daily 9am–5pm; April and Sept 9am–6pm; May–Aug 9am–7pm; Nov–Feb Sun 10am–5pm | cascata-varone. com* ▯▯ *J2*

2 TENNO & LAGO DI TENNO

12km to Lake Tenno north of Riva / 25 mins by car via the SS421

A winding road leads 6km uphill to Tenno, with vineyards to your right and the incredible views of Lake Garda to your left. As you arrive in the village, it's worth visiting the *Ristorante Castello (closed Wed | Via Castello 3 | tel. 04 64 50 06 38 | €),* where they serve excellent *carne salada* which originally comes from Tenno. You can take a delightful walk along the *Sentiero del Salt* to the *Canale di Tenno,* a well looked-after medieval village.

INSIDER TIP
More than carpaccio

If you drive on for a few kilometres, you get to the *Lago di Tenno,* a turquoise mountain lake with bathing beaches and an island. Ten years ago, this was a quiet Sunday excursion for local people. Today, while nature here is still pretty unspoilt, the beaches get crowded in summer. ▯▯ *J2*

3 LAGO DI LEDRO

14km west of Riva / 20 mins by car via the SS240

If it gets too hot or too crowded for you down on Lake Garda, you can take a

Hold on to your mobile in the Varone gorge

shortish trip into the mountains. Sporty types can go by mountain bike via the spectacular and scenic Sentiero Ponale, which is steep but offers wonderful lake views. On the high plain of the Ledro Valley *(vallediledro. com)* and on Lake Ledro, which is ideal for swimming, it is not only a few degrees cooler but there is also the 👓 *Museo delle Palafitte (March–June and Sept–Nov daily 9am–5pm; July/Aug 10am–6pm | 3.50 euros, up to 26 years of age 2.50 euros | Via al Lago 1 | palafitteledro.it)* in Molina di Ledro. The museum displays extraordinary finds from the peaty mud along the lake's shoreline – including ancient food leftovers! At the classy, rustic *Baita Santa Lucia (closed Mon | Via Santa Lucia 36 | Bezzecca | tel. 04 64 59 12 90 | vallediledro.com/baita | €€)*, you should try the typical Trentino specialities such as barley soup or home-made pasta. *□ H2*

TORBOLE

In summer, the small village of Torbole (stressed on the first 'o', pop. 900) is full of mountain bikers and surfers. This demographic also dominates the local nightlife and a lot of partying goes on!

Where previously there was only a handful of colourful fishing cottages in this idyllic spot between the lake and mountains, today hotels of all price groups are situated among the olive trees. The centre of the Old Town is small and easy to find one's way around. In winter, the streets are empty and many restaurants and hotels are closed.

SIGHTSEEING

CASA DEL DAZIO

The narrow, yellow 18th-century building in the small harbour is regarded by many as the emblem of Torbole. It is a former customs house as, until the end of World War I, this was the border between Austria and Italy. Unfortunately, it's not open to the public. *Via Benaco 26*

SANT'ANDREA

The uphill path is narrow and steep, but it is worth the effort because of the beautiful view over the lake. The 12th-century church used to be very simple but it was remodelled in the Baroque period. Presumably some of the locals sat as models for the realistic altarpiece. *Via della Chiesa 3*

EATING & DRINKING

BAR ALLA SEGA ⚑

The ultimate panoramic view! Guests who sit down to eat a *panino* shielded by the glass panel on the terrace can remove their pullovers in March and enjoy the view of the lake and mountains. *March–Oct daily 8.30am–midnight | Via Passsseggiata dell'Ora 1 | €*

CASA BEUST

In this restaurant by the lake tourists and local people eat side by side. The *sapori di lago*, a mixed hors d'oeuvre of Lake Garda fish and polenta slices, is a classic which you will remember for a long time. *Daily | Via Benaco 15 | tel. 04 64 50 63 25 | FB: Ristorante Pizzeria Casa Beust | €–€€*

INSIDER TIP
A special antipasto

PIZZA & BURGER

The address on Lake Garda for real Neapolitan pizza, i.e. with a thin base and thick edges. They also serve burgers. After dinner, you need to try their melon liquor! *Closed Wed | Via Matteotti 47 | tel. 04 64 90 51 77 | FB: Pizza&Burger Torbole | €*

SPORT & ACTIVITIES

SPORTS PARK & PANORAMIC TRAIL

In the sports park of  *Busatte Parco Avventura (see website for varying opening hours, mid-June–mid-Sept daily 10am–7pm | 18 euros, families 16 euros/pers., online discounts | busatteadventure.it)* high above Torbole, you can climb between trees on the high rope course and enjoy a 15m-high zipline (minimum height 1.45m for the zip-line and 1.25m for the high-rope course). A few steps further, you'll find the start of the panoramic trail from Busatte to Tempesta. Although this is not a fixed-rope route, clambering up and down metal ladders and steps in the cliff face does demand a head for heights. The return journey can be done by bus.

WINDSURFING

The *pelèr* wind from the north, the *ora* wind from the south and three other distinctive winds determine the life of the surfers in Torbole. There is a large selection of surf schools and places to hire boards, such as *Surf-Segnana (Foci del Sarca | surfsegnana.it)* or *Vasco Renna Surf (vascorenna.com).* The latter also offers fully equipped courses for children.

BEACHES

A long beach of small pebbles stretches from near the town centre to Monte Brione. On the *Spiaggia al Cor*, only five minutes from the town centre, children can have fun on the nearby playground. If you're after a sophisticated atmosphere, you can sunbathe directly beneath the slopes

Mediterranean atmosphere in an Alpine environment: windsurfer paradise Torbole of Monte Brione on the pebble beach of 🐦 *Baia Azzurra* in front of the hotel of the same name *(baia.it)* and drink a Spritz on a sofa at the hotel bar.

WELLNESS

Healing thermal waters bubble away in spa pools of the modern *Garda Thermae (see website for varying opening hours | Via Linfano 52 | garda thermae.it)*. It has three pools, various saunas, a beauty centre, a medical spa and a fitness room.

NIGHTLIFE

After the sun goes down, the nightlife scene takes to bar-hopping. First stop is *Aurora Bar (Via Matteotti 55)* in the Aurora Hotel with its colourful bean-bag seats. Then it's on to trendy *Wind's Bar (Via Matteotti 9)*, where you can drink cocktails and long drinks by the street until late at night. If you prefer a glass of wine in a quiet location, let the young owners of the *Vineria Refòl (Piazza Alpini 8)* advise you and enjoy the free olives and crisps.

AROUND TORBOLE

◢ NAGO

2km northeast of Torbole / 5 mins by bus route 3

A steep road, which is busy in summer, leads uphill from Torbole to Nago. If you prefer a quiet walk, you can hike through the Santa Lucia Valley past rock-climbing sites, rock terraces and olive trees. This trail, which was in use as early as Roman times, starts in Via di Santa Lucia. Beginning at the Hotel Santa Lucia, it will take you approx. one hour to Nago. **INSIDER TIP** **Prepare for a photo frenzy** Photographers should schedule an hour and a half because there are countless incredible lake views en route. In 1439, the track was used by the Venetians to carry six galleys and 25 other boats (which had been dismantled for easier transport) to Torbole in order to support the city of Brescia in its war with Milan.

In Nago, which is a continuation of Torbole, you can see the ruins of *Castello Penede*. The castle was destroyed by French troops around 1700 due to its strategically important location. From Nago castle, a path with panoramic views leads to the restored ruins of the fortress. ▯▯ J2

◢ MONTE BRIONE

2.5km northwest of Torbole / 45 mins via the hiking trail

Torbole and Riva are separated by the massive 376m-high limestone bluff of Monte Brione. Waymarked trails lead to the top. Until 1919, the Trentino belonged to Austria, and Monte Brione was on the border between the two countries. The most **INSIDER TIP** **An unusual viewpoint** remarkable viewpoint of Lake Garda is from the summit – on top of a bunker built by the Austrians in 1860. ▯▯ J2

6 MARMITTE DEI GIGANTI

30 mins north of Torbole via a hiking trail

Whether the Marmitte dei Giganti look like huge cauldrons from which giants quench their thirst – as the name implies – is a matter of conjecture. Whatever you want to believe, these glacial hollows – formed in the ice age – are impressive. Water from melting snow mixed with sand and gravel swirled around at great speed and scooped out these dips in the rock. You can get there via a 30-minute hiking trail which starts behind the Hotel Vela and leads along the Via Strada Granda. The sometimes extreme overhanging cliffs are popular with climbers. 📖 *J2*

7 ARCO

6km north of Torbole / 20 mins by bicycle along the River Sarca

Holidaymakers and mountain sports fans who prefer more peaceful surroundings head to the small town of Arco (pop. 18,000) with its historic centre that sits below a castle atop a massive cliff. To the north of the castle, the 300m-high Colodri wall is part of a legendary climbing area with a via ferrata. Local mountain guide groups offer guided tours, canyoning and climbing lessons. The mountaineering school *Mmove (Via Legionari Cecoslovacchi 14 | tel. 33 81 93 33 74 | mmove.net)* offers a two-hour 👹 climbing course for children several times a week.

We recommend that you start the day with a cappuccino: climbers meet in the Palazzo Marchetti at the *Ai Conti*

Arco's legendary Colodri wall

d'Arco (closed Thu | Piazza Prospero Marchetti 3 | aicontiarco.it), while mountain bikers prefer the *Caffè Trentino (Piazza III Novembre 10 | caffetrentino.com)*. Then you can stroll along the pedestrianised Via Segantini with its many sport shops, bars and ice cream parlours – *Tarifa (Via Giovanni Segantini 51)* being one of the best. *Via Ferrera* (parallel to Via Segantini) is quieter. Here, Antonio works away in his *La Primula (Via*

Ferrera 1) shop where he turns leather into beautiful bags, wallets, belts and shoes. Everything is handmade, which is why his ware is more expensive; but it will last you a lifetime.

Next, walk through lovely olive groves up to ★ *Castello di Arco (daily 10am–4pm, April–Sept until 7pm).* 🐗 You do not have to pay an entrance fee unless you want to explore past the jousting area with its amazing views. On the way back, stop at *Parco Arciducale (April–Sept daily 8am–7pm; Oct–March 9am–4pm).* This botanical garden with its more than 150 trees and shrubs, including some exotic species, was planted under the aegis of the Habsburg archduke from 1872.

On the way back to the town centre, you will go past a casino, which used to be frequented by European aristocracy and is where Austrian Empress Sisi once danced. Slightly outside the town centre, on the way to Riva, people meet at happy hour in the *Sol & Luna (Via Santa Caterina 40).* Order an aperitif and enjoy 🐗 free *panini*, bacon or pasta from the buffet. If you like vegetarian food, book a table at the vegan restaurant *Veganima (closed Wed | Viale Magnolie 29 | tel. 04 64 519764 | veganima.com | €).*

The bicycle paths along the River Sarca are wonderful. In approx. 20 minutes you can get to Torbole in the south while 20 minutes to the north with take you to Dro. And if you feel hungry along the way, in the hamlet of *La Moletta* on the bike path to Dro, the Baroni brothers run the kiosk of *Per Matteo (daily 11am–11pm | Località Moletta | FB: Chiosco per Matteo | €).* Here, locals order their sandwiches with *carne salada* and braised onions.

INSIDER TIP
Sandwich in local style

◾8 MAROCCHE DI DRO

15km north of Torbole / 45–60 mins along the Sarca bike path

A beautiful bike tour leads from Torbole to the spectacular rocky desert that was formed near Dro during the last ice age. You can trace dinosaur evidence on some of the rocks. Between Dro and Pietramurata, children and adolescents can enjoy climbing rocks and traversing high-rope courses in the 🧗 *Elias Adventure Park (June–Sept daily 10am–6.30pm | 8–17 euros depending on the chosen route | located in Gaggiolo 2 | elias adventurepark.com).* If you are brave enough, try the 200-m-long zip-line across the park and River Sarca. 🕮 *K1*

MALCESINE

(🕮 J4) **Welcome to one of the most romantic small towns on the lake. Narrow cobbled lanes lead to the old harbour and in the evening residents and tourists drink an** *aperitivo* **in one of the many squares or stroll alongside the harbour.**

Malcesine (pop. 3,700) is a very popular resort, but its atmosphere in the town centre has remained relaxed. Above the medieval Old Town towers the Scaliger castle, landmark of the

Stroll through Malcesine's Old Town and enjoy cobbled lanes and small shops

town. Malcesine is also the ideal starting point for excursions to Monte Baldo, either on foot or by cable car. The different quarters of Malcesine, from Navene to Cassone, are connected by 🐷 shuttle bus services *(visitmalcesine.com)* that run daily until late in the evening and cost only 1 euro per journey: highly recommended, especially on market days.

SIGHTSEEING

PALAZZO DEI CAPITANI DEL LAGO
If you find the hustle and bustle of the Old Town too much, this palace by the harbour is much quieter. It was built by the Scaligers in the 13th century – the unmistakable design of the battlements was borrowed from the Venetians. Nowadays it serves as the Town Hall where exhibitions are held from time to time. You should then visit the small palm garden directly on the lake where you can relax in peace and quiet. *Via Capitanato 2/4*

INSIDER TIP
Escape the crowds

CASTELLO SCALIGERO ★ ⚑
Don't miss a visit to Malcesine's Scaliger castle: the views are fantastic and the castle *museum* has been carefully modernised at great expense. The Goethe Room has copies of his drawings of Lake Garda. Goethe unpacked his paints and brushes inside the castle and nearly got arrested as a result: he was taken for a Habsburg spy who was not only interested in the castle's appearance but

also in its use as a military stronghold. When he told the guards he was from Frankfurt, everything turned out well. *April–Oct daily 9.30am–6pm; Nov–March varying opening times*

EATING & DRINKING

AGRITURISMO SAN MICHELE CA' DEL TOCIO

Located not far from the middle station of the Monte Baldo cable car, we recommend that you come here to check out the lake views as well as their delicious *primi*, for example truffle tagliatelle or risotto with gorgonzola. *Varying opening hours and days | Via San Michele 31 | tel. 34 42 67 76 74 | FB: Agriturismo San Michele Malcesine Cà del Tocio | €*

RE LEAR

One of the classier places to eat in Malcesine. You sit under a vaulted ceiling; it's more cosy than rustic and overlooks the little square to the front. The gourmet *table d'hôte* costs 50 euros and is money well spent. *Apart from peak season closed Tue | Piazza Cavour 23 | tel. 04 57 40 06 16 | FB: Re Lear Ristorante Malcesine | €€€*

SPECKSTUBE

The traditional-style Speckstube with its self-service beer garden is down-to-earth and family friendly. It is also very popular among the locals, offering a change from the many typical Italian restaurants. Kids can run about the playground. *Daily April–Oct | Via Navene Vecchia 139 | tel. 04 57 40 11 77 | speckstube.com | €*

A tandem flight from Monte Baldo will get your adrenaline pumping

SHOPPING

CONSORZIO OLIVICOLTORI

550 smallholders from Malcesine send their olives here for processing. The *shop (Via Navene 21)* also stocks other local products. If

INSIDER TIP
The secrets of olive oil

you book by Thursday noon, you can take part in a *guided tour* including oil tasting on Fridays at 10am. *(March–early Oct | Via Panoramica 232 | tel. 04 56 57 04 19). oliomalcesine.it*

MARKET

Every Saturday morning in the square by the Municipio.

SPORT & ACTIVITIES

MOUNTAIN BIKING

There is a business renting mountain bikes (from 25 euros/day) at the bottom of the cable car: *Xtreme (Via Navene Vecchia 10 | tel. 04 57 40 01 05 | xtrememalcesine.com).*

PARAGLIDING

Paragliders take off from below the top station, more info available from *Paragliding Malcesine (Via Gardesana 228 | tel. 33 56 11 29 02 | paragliding malcesine.it).* Tandem flights can be booked with the flying school *Fly 2 Fun (tel. 33 49 46 97 57 | tandem paragliding.eu).*

BEACHES

A safe footpath and cycle path leads to Navene, 5km to the north, so the beaches are easy to reach. Only 100m from the town centre is the popular pebble beach 🏖 *Spiaggia Paina.* There is also the tiny bathing cove of Posterna beneath the castle, plus a sunbathing area south of the promenade.

NIGHTLIFE

Malcesine's Old Town is bursting with life in summer until midnight.

OSTERIA SANTO CIELO

A small osteria where you can get light dishes, for example *bruschette* or a cheese platter, but the extensive wine list is more notable. Dutch owner Hella came to Italy because she fell in love and stayed on because of the cuisine. *Daily 10am–10pm | Piazza Turazza 11 | tel. 34 87 45 13 45| osteriasantocielo.com*

PUB VAGABONDO

Here, cyclists and kitesurfers exchange banter about wind and wild rides until 2am. Lots of locals, too. *Easter–Oct daily 9am–2am | Via Porta Orientale 1 | FB: Pub il Vagabondo*

AROUND MALCESINE

🟩 FUNIVIA MALCESINE-MONTE BALDO ⭐ 🚩

The Monte Baldo cable car climbs 1,700m from Malcesine via the middle station of San Michele to the summit.

Enjoy 360-degree panoramic views of Monte Baldo from the *funivia* and the mountains

That's a double treat since you get a lot of time to look at the view as well as a ride. The cabins are glazed all round and turn on their own axis. As this is a very popular excursion, on some days you should expect long queues! The only way to avoid the crowds is to get up early and catch one of the first cable cars of the morning, before the crowds arrive.

INSIDER TIP
Arrivederci, queuing!

Alternatively, book a Fast Ticket online which gives you direct access to the departure zone. Mountain bikes may also be taken to the middle station, but only at specified times.

Once at the top, mountain bikers and hikers can choose from a variety of panoramic paths with all degrees of difficulty. A particular treat is the hike to the Monte Altissimo and the *Rifugio Altissimo Damiano Chiesa (tel. 04 64 86 71 30 | rifugioaltissimo.it | €)*, which takes about four hours. The view from the peak is a fitting reward for the effort, and lodge-keeper Eleonora Orlandi serves up local specialities. If you don't like hiking on your own, book a tour at *Elalpaca (Azienda Agricola Elalpaca | tel. 33 31 62 35 71 | elalpaca.it)* with an unexpected companion: 🦙 With alpacas on the lead and a guide, you can set off every day at 9am and 2.30pm. This is great fun, and not just for children, especially during the "mini trekking" in the afternoon. You need to book the tour by 6pm on the evening before.

The *Baita dei Forti (daily | tel. 04 57 40 03 19 | baitadeiforti.com | €–€€)* is a restaurant near the summit of the cable car. Dishes include the *Trittico Baldo* – a spicy trio of venison goulash, mushroom ragout and grilled cheese. You can also stay the night in one of the six rooms. *Uphill cable car rides daily 8am–4pm 5pm and 6pm, depending on the season; downhill rides 8.15am–4.45pm, 5.45pm and 6.45pm | depending on the season/ day of the week, return fare 15–22 euros, one-way 10–15 euros, with a mountain bike 15 euros | funivie delbaldo.it ⊞ J4*

🔟 EREMO SANTI BENIGNO E CARO

2 hrs south of Malcesine on the hiking trail from the cable car's middle station

The hermitage of the Blessed Benignus and Carus is in Cassone. It can be reached via a two-hour walk from the middle station of the cable car from Malcesine. The path is signposted and easy to find. The church is only open on a few days each year. Processions from Malcesine take place on 12 April, 27 July, 16 August and on the third Sunday in October. ⊞ J4

🔢 BRENZONE & CASSONE

10km to Castelletto south of Malcesine / 15 mins via the Gardesana Orientale

If you head south along the lake, it's not far to *Cassone* and then to *Brenzone*, which is really a collection of villages between Malcesine and Torri del Benaco. The source of the River Aril is in picturesque Cassone. The river only runs for about 175m before it flows into the lake. Although promoted by the locals and tempting to believe, it is actually not the shortest river in the world. In the small harbour there is the free 🐷 *Museo del Lago (Tue–Sun, in winter only Sun 10am–noon and 3–6pm)*, the carefully renovated fishermen's museum.

The numerous villages of Brenzone are scattered around the foot of Monte Baldo. This means there are many trekking routes and downhill trails for hikers and mountain bikers. For example, you can only reach the picturesque medieval village of *Campo*, which 230m up in a remote location in the middle of centuries-old olive groves, via a steep hiking path that begins in Castelletto di Brenzone. The village houses don't have running water. However, if Signora Olga is at home, she will offer hikers an espresso or a glass of grappa – simply ask the residents for Olga!

INSIDER TIP
Grappa instead of acqua

After the hike, treat yourself to dinner at the *Osteria al Pescatore (closed Mon and at lunchtime | Via Imbarcadero 31 | tel. 04 57 43 07 02 | osteriaalpescatore.it | €€)* in Castelletto di Brenzone (book in advance!). Don't ask for the menu because there is none: Mamma Rosaria and her daughter Sara will cook up a five-course menu with the catch of the day. Restaurant owner Lino entertains the room with a loudspeaker and entertaining stories from the past. ⊞ H–J 4–5

EASTERN SHORE

OLD TOWN LANES & AMUSEMENT PARKS

The eastern shore of the lake is known as the "Olive Riviera": the trees' silvery leaves catch the sunlight and stretch as far as the eye can see. For olive-growers the harvest season is late autumn. Everybody helps – adults and young children alike; depending on how ripe they are, the green or black olives are shaken from the trees using sticks and other special devices. The fruits are collected by hand, as they always have been. And those who have no olive trees are likely to cultivate vines instead.

Torri del Benaco: if you arrive by ferry, it will look as if you are sailing towards the castle

The eastern shore is easy to explore using the lakeside *Gardesana Orientale*. This narrow road runs from Torbole in the north via Torri del Benaco, which is grouped around the old harbour, to busy Garda, then Bardolino, the biggest town on the eastern shore, and on to the small medieval town of Lazise. It is a delightful tour offering plenty of cultural attractions, several Scaliger castles and wonderful Venetian *palazzi*. However, you should leave plenty of time for this trip, as during peak season the *Gardesana Orientale* gets very busy.

EASTERN SHORE

Muslone

Gargnano

Castelletto

Navazzo

Carpeneda

Pai di Sotto

Grotta Tanella `2`

Vobarno

Collio

Maderno

Toscolano-

Lago

San Zeno di Montagna `6`

Roè

Volciano

Gardone Riviera

Albisano `1`

Tormini

`45`

Salò

Torri del Benaco p.64 ●━━━`1`━━ Albisano

Soprazocco

Castion

Verone

San Felice
del Benaco

Rock engravings `4`
Cimitero
Militare Tedesco `5`

Baia
delle Sirene

Punta San Vigilio ★ `3`

Garda p.6 ●

Muscoline

Puegnago
sul Garda

Solarolo

Spiaggia
del Corno

`9` Eremo
San Giorg

Bardolin ●
p.71

Polpenazze del Garda

Piazza Giacomo Matteotti ★ ●

Soiano del Lago

Moniga del Garda

di Garda

Cisano

`10` Museo
dell'Olio di Oliva

Padenghe
sul Garda

1 hr 10 mins

Lazise ●
p.76

1 hr

Desenzano del Garda

Colombare

Colà

Pacengo

Lonato del Garda

Lugana

San Benedetto di Lugana

Sirmione

Castelnuc
del Gar

`49`

`11` Peschiera del Garda

Esenta

Broglie

LOMBARDIA

`567`

Ponti sul Mincio

Salionze

Pozzolengo

Castiglione delle Stiviere

Monzambano

`236`

Solferino

Castellaro Lagusello

Valeggio sul Mincio `249`

5 km
3.11 mi

Cavriana

Valeggio & Borghetto sul Mincio `12`

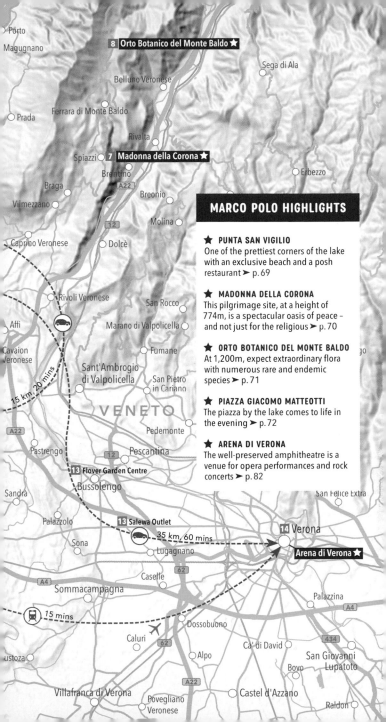

8 Orto Botanico del Monte Baldo ★

Sega di Ala

○ Porto Magugnano

Belluno Veronese

Ferrara di Monte Baldo

○ Prada

Rivalta

Erbezzo ○

Spiazzi **7** Madonna della Corona ★

Brentino

A22

Braga

Breonio

Vilmezzano ○

Molina

Caprino Veronese

○ Dolcè

Rivoli Veronese

San Rocco

Affi

Marano di Valpolicella

Cavaion Veronese

Fumane

Sant'Ambrogio di Valpolicella

San Pietro in Cariano

VENETO

Pedemonte

A22

Pastrengo

Pescantina

12

13 Flover Garden Centre

Bussolengo

Sandra

San Felice Extra

Palazzolo

13 Salewa Outlet

Sona

35 km, 60 mins

Lugagnano

14 Verona

Arena di Verona ★

Caselle

62

Sommacampagna

A4

Palazzina

15 mins

A4

Dossobuono

Caluri

62

Ca' di David

434

Alpo

San Giovanni Lupatoto

○ustoza

Bovo

A22

Villafranca di Verona

Povegliano Veronese

Castel d'Azzano

Raldon ○

15 km, 20 mins

MARCO POLO HIGHLIGHTS

★ PUNTA SAN VIGILIO
One of the prettiest corners of the lake with an exclusive beach and a posh restaurant ➤ p. 69

★ MADONNA DELLA CORONA
This pilgrimage site, at a height of 774m, is a spectacular oasis of peace – and not just for the religious ➤ p. 70

★ ORTO BOTANICO DEL MONTE BALDO
At 1,200m, expect extraordinary flora with numerous rare and endemic species ➤ p. 71

★ PIAZZA GIACOMO MATTEOTTI
The piazza by the lake comes to life in the evening ➤ p. 72

★ ARENA DI VERONA
The well-preserved amphitheatre is a venue for opera performances and rock concerts ➤ p. 82

TORRI DEL BENACO

(□ H6) **The best and most practical way to get to Torri del Benaco (pop. 3,000) from the west is to take the ferry from Maderno – unless you feel like driving halfway round the lake to visit the opposite shore.**

From the lake, it is clear to see how the ⚑ Scaliger Castle dominates the town. The fortress dates back to the ninth century and, in 1383, the Scaliger ruler Antonio della Scala, had it converted into a residence. During renovation work in the 20th century, a pink-coloured marble plaque was discovered in the castle. The plaque bears a carved relief of the Scaliger coat-of-arms – a "scale" in the form of a ladder with five rungs, now on show in the museum. Today, the castle is a best-kept secret among engaged couples as civil ceremonies can be performed there (*torri-del-benaco.net*). The tower with its view of the lake and the *Limonaie* (lemon glasshouse) are particularly romantic locations.

Torri del Benaco is one of the quieter places on the eastern shore, not nearly as overrun as its neighbours Garda or Bardolino. It has probably the most picturesque harbour on the lake, which stretches right into the town itself; in the oval-shaped harbour small, brightly coloured fishing boats bob up and down. The countryside beyond Torri del Benaco is not as steep as elsewhere because Monte Baldo is slightly further away from the lake at this point.

SIGHTSEEING

MUSEO DEL CASTELLO SCALIGERO

The folk museum in Scaliger Castle provides a good insight of how the people on Lake Garda used to live before the tourists arrived, earning their living primarily from fishing and the olive industry. The displays on boat building and local rock engravings are particularly interesting. Visitors to the museum can also see the *Limonaie* (lemon glasshouse) built in 1760 – the only one on the eastern shore that is still in use today. *Mid-June–mid-Sept daily 9.30am–1pm and 4.30–7.30pm; April–mid-Jun and mid-Sept–Oct 9.30am–12.30pm and 2.30–6pm except Mon 2.30–6pm | Viale Fratelli Lavanda 2 | museodel castelloditorridelbenaco.it*

SANTISSIMA TRINITÀ

Small but beautiful – the little church by the harbour originates from the 14th century and accommodates renovated frescos by the school of Giotto, *the* Renaissance painter in Northern Italy.

SANTI PIETRO E PAOLO

The large church organ of 1744, which is still used, is an unusual one to find in Italy. Another unusual feature in this Baroque church is the bronze statue of the priest Giuseppe Nascimbeni, who was beatified in 1988. Nascimbeni founded the charitable convent in Torri. *parrochiadi torridelbenaco.it*

It looks romantic but it's hard work: olive harvest near Torri

EATING & DRINKING

ALLA GROTTA

You cannot get closer to the lake: with the sound of babbling water on the small terrace above the lake, the fish and pizza taste three times as good. *Daily | Corso Dante Alighieri 61 | tel. 34 77 60 60 00 | €€*

LE GEMME DI ARTEMISIA

Have you always wondered how to make tortellini? Or how top Italian chefs make truffle risotto? If the answer is yes, then you should sign up for a cooking lesson with Chef Andrea Messini from Le Gemme di Artemisia. Alongside his restaurant business – only a single table with a surprise menu – in Albisano, he also shares the secrets of his craft with those who are interested.

INSIDER TIP
Learn from a top chef

You need to book the one table in advance, and for 100 euros you get a classy five-course menu. *Albisano | Via Corrubio 18 | tel. 04 52 42 86 22 | legemmediartemisia.it | €€€*

TRATTORIA LONCRINO

Only 500m from the centre, in Loncrino, you can tuck into local food served in a relaxed atmosphere and enjoy a view of the lake from the terrace. *Daily | Via Pirandello 10 | located in Loncrino | tel. 04 56 29 00 18 | FB: Trattoria Loncrino | €–€€*

SHOPPING

ARTS & CRAFTS MARKET

At the height of summer, artists and craftspeople set up their stalls in the Old Town centre every Thursday evening.

MARKET

Every Monday morning a market is held on the road along the shore.

SPORT & ACTIVITIES

Tra gli Olivi i Tesori di Torri del Benaco, "Between the olive trees, the treasures of Torri" is the name of a hiking trail that will take you to nine little churches in the area.

BEACHES

A long beach (free access) can be found at the southern end of the village; a few willow trees offer a little shade.

NIGHTLIFE

Torri nightlife is picturesque, with both young and old meeting at *Don Diego (Vicolo Fosse 7 | dondiegotorri.it)* to drink sangria and eat from platters of delicious hors d'oeuvres. Film showings take place in the new theatre in summer.

AROUND TORRI DEL BENACO

🚹 ALBISANO

2km east of Torri / 45 mins on foot via the hiking trail

A waymarked footpath (pretty steep) will take you up to this village, which clings to the ridge of Monte Baldo.

You'll be gasping anyway when you get to the top – the view from the terrace of the parish church is breathtakingly beautiful. *H6*

🚹 GROTTA TANELLA

6km north of Torri / 10 mins via the Gardesana Orientale

Head to the north to Pai di Sopra for the caves of "Grotta Tanella" – which lead about 400m deep into the rocky cliff of Monte Baldo – and admire the stalactites and stalagmites. This is a genuine alternative to the usual beach routine. The guided tour is accompanied by experts of the association *Biosphaera (Piazza San Marco | tel. 34 07 66 11 16 | biosphaera.it). H5*

GARDA

(H6) **Garda has a population of 4,000 and stretches around the wide bay between Punta San Vigilio and the Rocca.**

The pretty, traffic-free Old Town is a popular place to stroll among locals and tourists alike. The shore is lined with one café after another. The lanes in the Old Town are quite narrow and the main streets can get very crowded at times. However, if you get away from the shops there are still secret corners to be discovered. In the evening things quieten down and you can sit cosily in the cafés along Lungolago Regina Adelaide.

As early as CE 768, Charlemagne had made Garda a county in its own right, and from then on the lake was named after this town, and not by its earlier Roman name of Benacus.

In addition to the Old Town with the many sympathetically restored *palazzi*, the lush countryside surrounding Garda is a visitor attraction, and nature lovers delight in the Mediterranean vegetation. Old monasteries, farms and country houses are tucked away on the hillside slopes and can be explored on longer hiking tours.

SIGHTSEEING

SANTA MARIA MAGGIORE

Garda's parish church is outside the original town walls. It is presumed that the earlier structure on the site, built by the Lombards in the eighth century, was the fortress chapel, as the site is directly below the Rocca. The 15th-century cloisters are well worth seeing. *Piazzale Roma*

ROCCA DI GARDA

The Rocca di Garda is a hill that rises about 300m above the eastern shore. From the top, you can enjoy an amazing view over Garda and Punta San Vigilio. Although the area is now covered in forest, a thousand years ago it was the site of a fortress in which Queen Adelaide of Burgundy was held captive. All that remains of the castle today are a few stones, but children queue to have their picture taken in front of 👯 "Adelaide's throne", which is really a giant rock. A well-marked trail leads up to the castle from behind the Santa Maria Maggiore church.

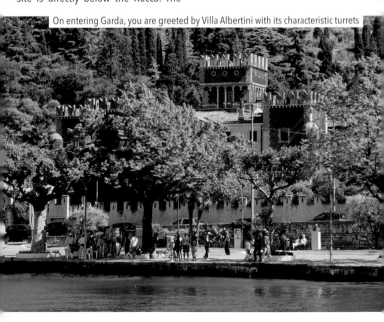

On entering Garda, you are greeted by Villa Albertini with its characteristic turrets

VILLA ALBERTINI

The dark red villa at the northern town entrance, with its distinctive crenellated Ghibelline-style towers, cannot be missed. It can only be viewed from the outside.

AI BEATI

This restaurant is in a stunning location at the top of the hill and offers exclusive cuisine, but at a price! Those looking for a memorable evening in an exclusive setting – no shorts and sandals, please – will definitely be happy here. *Daily | Via Val Mora 57 | tel. 04 57 25 57 80 | ristoranteaibeati.com | €€€*

OSTERIA AL VICOLO

Would you like an unpretentious but delicious supper? This osteria in the Old Town serves Lake Garda classics such as home-made *bigoli con le sarde* or *con il luccio* (with pike!) at reasonable prices. *Daily | Via XX Settembre 23 | tel. 35 15 50 16 01 | FB: Osteria al Vicolo | €*

REGIO PATIO

Prepare yourself for a culinary experience. The menu in the gourmet restaurant of the Regina Adelaide Hotel changes in line with the seasons, and more than 200 wines are stored in the cellar. *Daily | Via San Francesco d'Assisi 23 | tel. 04 57 25 59 77 | regina-adelaide.it | €€€*

COOPERATIVA FRA PESCATORI ⚑

Fresh fish can be bought from the local fishing cooperative. *Daily 6.30am–12.30pm | Via San Bernardo 79 | coopgarda.it*

Blow the budget and treat yourself to a night in the Locanda San Vigilio

LA BOTTEGA DELLA PASTA

This shop in Costermano, 4km east of Garda, is all about pasta: what is normal for Italian housewives is a mini-attraction for many tourists – a shop with exclusively fresh home-made pasta. Among the specialities of the store are stuffed tortellini and *tortelli*, which vary depending on the season. *Costermano | Via San Giuseppe Artigiano 2b*

INSIDER TIP
Seasonal pasta

MARKET

Every Friday morning there is a market on *Lungolago Regina Adelaide*.

SPORT & ACTIVITIES

In Marciaga, 2km north of Garda, you will find a very well-maintained 18-hole golf course as well as a large climbing area with many light routes rated up to 6a nestled in the hills covered with vineyards and olive trees. At the 🐾 🍴 *Gardacqua (Mon–Fri 9am–9.30pm, Sat 9am–9pm, Sun 9am–8pm | day ticket 10.70 euros, Sat/Sun 12.30 euros, children under 14 years 8.10 and 9.30 euros | Via Cirillo Salaorni 10 | gardacqua.org)* you can have fun in interior and exterior pools with water slides and games.

BEACHES

Between Garda and Punta San Vigilio is the long, narrow pebble beach of 🌴 *Spiaggia del Corno*. No entrance fee, but there are very few parking spaces.

NIGHTLIFE

ART CAFE ALLA TORRE

Exhibitions are held in cooperation with the Cerchio Aperto Cultural Association at this special location as well as the occasional open-air concert organised in conjunction with the restaurant Giardino delle Rane. *Daily 7am–midnight | Piazza Calderini 1 | ilgiardinodellerane.com*

PAPILLON

Live music is sometimes played in this bar well into the night. *Wed–Mon 6pm–3am | Via delle Antiche Mura 22*

AROUND GARDA

🔳 PUNTA SAN VIGILIO ⭐

3km west of Garda / 40 mins on foot via the shoreline trail

This peninsula lies immediately to the west of Garda. An extensive olive grove follows the curve of the lovely bay – the 🌴 🐾 *Baia delle Sirene (parcobaia dellesirene.it)*, where you can bathe – at a price *(entrance fee 12 euros)*. There is also a children's activity programme *(6 euros)*. In 1540, Michele Sanmicheli – an accomplished builder of fortresses – constructed the *Villa Guarienti-Brenzone* on the peninsula. Those who can afford it stay at the *Locanda San Vigilio (locanda-sanvigilio.it)*. Visitors on a more modest budget can at least enjoy a cappuccino or Campari here. *📖 G6*

4 ROCK ENGRAVINGS

1¾ hrs north of Garda via the hiking trail

Please note, the engravings carved into the rock face here are 3,000 years old. Presumably, it was shepherds who left their artistic mark here at the foot of Monte Baldo and especially on Monte Luppia in the bay of Garda. There are engravings of ships, riders, warriors and lances. From Punta San Vigilio, a trail with route markers and information boards leads uphill under olive trees, hornbeams and ash trees to Monte Luppia. *H6*

5 CIMITERO MILITARE TEDESCO

4km east of Garda / approx. 10 mins via the SP8

Further inland near Garda and south of Costermano is the *Cimitero Militare Tedesco*, the largest military cemetery for German soldiers in Italy. Almost 22,000 Germans are laid to rest here. They were killed in Northern Italy during World War II. A controversy erupted when it became known that not only victims, but also perpetrators were buried at the cemetery. The following notice is therefore displayed on an information board: "At this cemetery lie the mortal remains of those who were also actively responsible for war crimes. Their crimes will always be a warning to us." *H6*

6 SAN ZENO DI MONTAGNA

12km north of Garda / 20 mins via Costermano and Castion Veronese

A beautiful panoramic route takes you from Garda via Costermano to San Zeno, 560m high up the mountain. In summer, nature lovers are drawn here, while gastronomes arrive in the autumn when the chestnuts are ripe and ready to feature as starters, side dishes or desserts. Treat yourself to the mouth-watering specialities at the exceptional *Taverna Kus (Nov–Feb, closed Mon–Wed | located at Castello 14 | tel. 04 57 28 56 67 | ristorante veronatavernakus.it | €€–€€€)*.

In the *Caseificio Baldo Garda (Via Zanetti 2 | caseificiobaldogarda.it)* you just have to try the delicious *ubriaco*, the "drunk" cheese which is left to mature in the pomace of the premium red wine Amarone for 30 days. Above San Zeno, in the 🎭 *Jungle Adventure Park (May–Sept daily 10am–6pm | 8–34 euros depending on the chosen course | Pineta Sperane | jungleadventurepark.com)* you can climb through the treetops on wooden walkways. *H5*

INSIDER TIP
Drunk cheese

7 MADONNA DELLA CORONA ⭐

22km northeast of Garda / 30 mins via the SP11 to Brentino, then on foot via the pilgrimage trail

One of the most picturesque and spectacular sites on Lake Garda is this pilgrimage church 774m above the Adige Valley. In the 15th century, the church was built right into the cliff that towers above the village of Spiazzi. If you are up for it, you can hike two hours up the steep pilgrimage path from Brentino on the eastern side of Monte Baldo to the santuario. *madonnadellacorona.it* *J5*

🟦 ORTO BOTANICO DEL MONTE BALDO ★ ⚑

30km northeast of Garda / 50 mins via the SP8

Over 600 plant species grow on the slopes of Monte Baldo, including several botanical rarities. Many refer to these botanical gardens as the "Garden of Europe". At a height of 1,200m near Novezzina, it houses an extraordinary collection of plants, many of which are endemic to the area. *Opens about 2 weeks after the snow melts until the onset of winter, daily, 9am–sunset | guided tours by appointment, tel. 04 56 24 72 88 | ortobotanicomontebaldo.org 🗺 J5*

BARDOLINO

(🗺 H6) **This place name may ring a bell even if you've never been to Lake Garda: Bardolino is also the name of the wine that grows on the gentle slopes rising up behind the little town which lies towards the southern end of the eastern shore.**

The area was settled back in the Bronze Age. Later, the Romans built a town which developed into the self-governing community of Bardolino in the Middle Ages, when it came under the rule of the House of Scaliger. The Old Town in Bardolino (pop. 7,100) is larger than that of other towns along the "Olive Riviera". The shops in the relatively wide lanes that criss-cross each other stay open until around

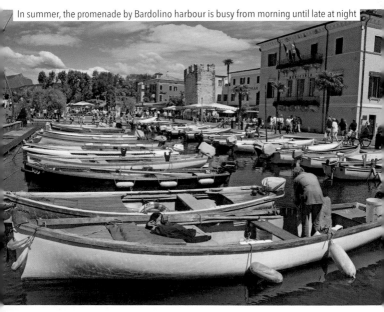
In summer, the promenade by Bardolino harbour is busy from morning until late at night

San Severo's simple style is free from any pompous decor

midnight. But the throngs of visitors only arrive during the summer months. In September, it is already noticeably more peaceful and atmospheric.

SIGHTSEEING

PIAZZA GIACOMO MATTEOTTI ★

Bardolino's main square is always brimming with life. It is in fact a wide street that leads from the neoclassical parish church of San Nicolò down to the lakeside. This is where you'll find a number of bars, cafés and ice cream parlours. And it is where locals and holidaymakers come to stroll in the evenings: *fare le vasche* as the Italians call it – "doing lengths".

VILLAS

Bardolino has an aristocratic air. A walk past these noble residences will take you back to past centuries. The *Villa Guerrieri Rizzardi* with its (private) park (which belongs to the winery of the same name) is the middle of the Old Town centre. The *Villa Carrara Bottagisio* now houses the town library and has a public park, and is right next to the yellow-coloured *Villa delle Magnolie* (private) and the *Villa delle Rose*, which is also a private estate.

SAN SEVERO

The small church on the main road was rebuilt in the Romanesque style after the earthquake of 1117. The remains of the previous church, some 300 years older, can still be seen. Particularly beautiful are the faded but largely intact 12th-century frescos that once covered the whole interior of this harmoniously designed church.

MUSEO DEL VINO ☂

On the family estate, Gaetano Zeni runs a wine museum where the wine-making process is explained. In the *Galleria Olfattiva* you can test your sommelier's nose and see whether you recognise the various aromas. After you've toured the museum, wines are available for tasting and purchase. *Mid-March–Oct daily 9am–12.30pm and 2.30–7pm | Via Costabella 9 | museodelvino.it |* ⏱ *45 mins, incl. tasting 1½ hrs*

EATING & DRINKING

AL CARDELLINO

The Modena family takes good care of its guests. Mama Rosa makes the pasta (with truffles) by hand, but Papa Aldo is the fish expert. If you like pork, try their variation in a sesame crust. *Closed Tue and at lunchtime except for Sun | located in Cisano | Via Pralesi 16 | tel. 04 56 22 90 48 | alcardellino.it | €€–€€€*

IL GIARDINO DELLE ESPERIDI

In this restaurant, which is run exclusively by women, the menu is short but the dishes have something extra special, for example thinly cut bull meat, marinated and flash fried, or a tobacco ice cream for dessert. Booking is essential! *Closed Wed lunchtime*

BARDOLINO

73

and Tue | *Via Mameli 1* | *tel. 04 56 21 04 77* | *€€€*

LA VERANDA DEL COLOR
Here, a risotto with fresh cheese, peppers and liquorice costs 21 euros. But if you want to treat yourself while on holiday, la Veranda, with its Michelin star, is the right place! *Closed at lunchtime* | *Via Santa Cristina 5* | *tel. 04 56 21 08 57* | *ristorantelaveranda-abardolino.it* | *€€€*

RISTORANTE PIZZERIA CATULLO
In this restaurant, which belongs to the hotel of the same name, extremely friendly staff serve pizza from the wood-fired oven or traditional pasta and fish dishes. Extra special is the harbour view which you can enjoy from the outdoor tables. *Daily* | *Lungolago Francesco Lenotti 8* | *tel. 04 57 21 00 08* | *ristorantecatullo.it* | *€€*

VILLA CALICANTUS
Former banker Daniele quit his job in Paris to create one of the smallest wineries in the Bardolino area. He and his wife press organic wines and organize guided tours and generous tastings with home-made and regional products *(35 euros/person)*. *Calmasino di Bardolino* | *Via Concordia 13* | *tel. 34 03 66 67 40* | *villacalicantus.it*

SHOPPING

CANTINE LENOTTI ⚑
This family-run business has been a winery since 1906. Their excellent but not exactly cheap wine goes under the label "Decus", but they also have commendable table wines. *Via Santa Cristina 1* | *lenotti.it*

MARKET
The market – one of the biggest on the lake – is held at the promenade every Thursday from 8am to 1.30pm.

SPORT & ACTIVITIES

From Bardolino, a superb lake promenade leads north as far as Garda and south to Lazise. From north to south there are 10km for joggers, hikers and even skaters to enjoy and explore. Don't forget to take swimming gear, as there are plenty of beaches on the way! A suggested tour, which offers plenty of variety, will take you to Garda in one hour. As you leave the town, the route leaves the shoreline for a short period and heads inland. If you pass the red house, you are heading in the right direction! Some hotels rent bikes, otherwise enquire at *Tita Sport (Via Marconi 44* | *tel. 04 56 21 08 69* | *titasport.it)*.

BEACHES

There is no swimming in the town itself, but to the north and south of the Old Town there are several beaches along the shoreline. The place to swim nearest the town centre is 😎 *Punta Cornicello*. The small pebbly beach (free of charge) near Via Ugo Foscolo also has a children's playground. A good swimming option is to jump into the lake from a boat, or better still a ketch, which is a 19th-century

Piazza Matteotti: in summer, Bardolino's main square becomes an open-air concert venue

fishing boat. Maybe you're interested in a romantic cruise on the lake … At sunset you can enjoy a glass of prosecco on board the "San Nicolò".

INSIDER TIP
Prosecco at sunset

For more information about sailing trips visit *sannicolo1925.com* and book at *Europlan (tel. 04 56 20 94 44 | europlan.it)*.

WELLNESS

At the *Caesius Thermae & Spa Resort (Via Peschiera 3 | tel. 04 57 21 91 00 | hotelcaesiusterme.com)* in Cisano you can enjoy an introduction into the ancient art of Ayurveda.

NIGHTLIFE

BAR ZERO45
Cocktail fans will find a large selection in this bar. If you visit on 🐷 Sunday between 11am and 1pm and order an aperitif, you will get a traditional dish of food for free! *Via Mameli 10 | FB: Zero45 Bardolino*

CONCERTS 🐷
At 9.30pm every Wednesday in the summer season, classical concerts are given by the Bardolino Philharmonic Orchestra on the Piazza Matteotti in front of the parish church of San Nicolò.

HOLLYWOOD
House rhythms play in the *Main Room*, while live music can be heard in the *Privee*. Guests can also dine at the *Sinatra Restaurant* next to the pool. Ladies wearing high heels (at least 12cm) get in free of charge! *April–Oct Fri/Sat, July/Aug also Wed from 8.30pm | Via Montavoletta 11 | hollywood.it*

AROUND BARDOLINO

🟨 EREMO SAN GIORGIO

5km north of Bardolino / 10 mins via the SP.32

The Camaldolese hermitage has been a retreat since the 17th century for those in need, from monks to farmers. Nowadays, it is also a place of rest for anybody who wishes to escape the hectic pace of city life. You can request single rooms for overnight stays. Home-made organic products are on sale in the monastery shop. The honey, liqueurs and syrups are mouth-wateringly good. *Tel. 04 57 21 13 90 | eremosangiorgio.it ⊞ H6*

🔟 MUSEO DELL'OLIO DI OLIVA

2km south of Bardolino / approx. 5 mins towards Lazise

In Cisano, near Bardolino, the olive oil museum is the perfect place not just to buy quality oil straight from the producer but also to find out in depth how olive oil is manufactured. *Mon–Sat 9am–12.30pm and 2.30–7pm, Sun 9am–12.30pm | Via Peschiera 54 | museum.it | ⏱ 30 mins ⊞ H7*

1️⃣1️⃣ STRADA DEL VINO

8km to Affi east of Bardolino / 15 mins via Cavaion Veronese

This is a route that one person will not be able to enjoy very much: the driver… The "Wine Route" starts at Costermano just a little to the north of Bardolino and goes through Affi, Pastrengo and Castelnuovo in the direction of Peschiera. With more than 70 wineries, restaurants and places to stay along the road, you can enjoy, taste and buy all the wine you want. *bardolino-stradadelvino.it ⊞ H–J 6–8*

LAZISE

(⊞ H7) **The small town might seem as if it wants to ward off visitors: the 14th-century fortified walls around the Old Town of Lazise (pop. 7,000) are still fully intact, and you can only enter through three gateways.**

It is significantly quieter here than in any of the other places on the eastern shore and this makes the pretty town with its small harbour, the Scaliger Castle and the unusually large Piazza Vittorio Emanuele all the more attractive. Lazise was an important trading post under Venetian rule. A visible reminder of that time can be seen in the customs house at the harbour, from where Venice kept a watch on the trading of goods on the lake.

SIGHTSEEING

SAN NICOLÒ

Pause, light a candle and admire the beautifully restored frescoes created by the school of Giotto … The small Romanesque church is right on the harbourside and is worth a detour.

SCALIGER CASTLE 🚩

The castle dates from the 14th century and can only be viewed from the outside, as it is a private residence. It was fortified to protect the strategically important Lazise harbour.

TOWN WALL

The wall around the Old Town of Lazise has a historical explanation: Venice continually strengthened its outposts on Lake Garda against attacks from Milan. The town was accessible via three gates: the *Porta Nuova* in the north, *Porta San Zeno* in the direction of Gardesana and *Porta del Lion* in the south.

EATING & DRINKING

AL CASTELLO

Sitting in a large inner courtyard, right next to the town wall, guests can enjoy grilled trout or spaghetti with clams. *Closed Thu lunchtime | Via Porta del Lion 8 | tel. 04 52 47 72 32 | famigliabozzini.it | €€*

ALLA GROTTA

Connoisseurs appreciate the restaurant's exceptional and inspired (fish) cuisine by the small harbour. The best tables are outdoors with sea views. *Closed Tue | Via Francesco Fontana 8 | tel. 04 57 58 00 35 | allagrotta.it | €€*

CLASSIQUE

This 19th-century villa slightly above the lakeside promenade is one of the most beautifully situated restaurants on Lake Garda. You'll find the view across the water quite breathtaking. Inside, marvel at the floor mosaics. *Daily | Via Albarello 33 | tel. 04 57 58 02 70 | ristoclassique.it | €€*

COZZERIA ALLE MURA

Admittedly, mussels with gorgonzola may not be to everyone's taste. However, all 21 mussel variations served at this restaurant are delicious – whether exotic with citrus fruits,

Despite being 700 years old, Lazise's 14th-century town wall is in good condition

traditional with lemon and pepper or creative with gorgonzola or wheat beer. *Closed Mon | Via Cansignorio 16 | tel. 04 56 47 06 44 | cozzeria. com | €€*

GEM'S BREW PUB

INSIDER TIP
Craft beer all'italiana

The home-brewed, natural and unfiltered beer in this pub and pizzeria goes down well. It is popular among locals who like to sit at the rustic wooden tables outside or drink their beer in traditional pub style inside. *Daily | located in Praleor 25 | tel. 04 56 47 11 44 | gemsbrewpub.it | €*

extensive list of wines proves how appropriate the name is. *Via Cansignorio 10 | artedelbere.com*

MARKET

A market is held every Wednesday morning on *Lungolago Marconi*.

SPORT & ACTIVITIES

ADVENTURE PARKS

Approx. 3km south of Lazise in the 🐵 *Aquapark Caneva*, children can drift on rubber rings down the Lazy River while brave adults can climb a 32-m-high tower and throw themselves down a steep slide. If you

Lazise's Piazza Vittorio Emanuele is unusually big for a small town on Lake Garda

SHOPPING

ENOTECA L'ARTE DEL BERE

"The Art of Drinking" is the name of this *enoteca*, based on the notion that life is too short to drink poor wine. The

are looking for an even greater adrenalin rush, the neighbouring *Hollywoodpark Movieland* will make you feel like a real stuntman on the Hollywood Action Tower, where a free fall from a great height is simulated.

Visit their website for varying opening times | Movieland or Aquapark 28 euros, children under 1.40m tall 22 euros; combined ticket 35/29 euros, discounted tariffs online | canevaworld.it

But that's not all! Another 3km in the direction of Peschiera is the 🎭 Gardaland theme park *(visit their website for varying opening times | 40.50 euros, children under 10 years 34.50 euros | gardaland.it)* with attractions for all age groups. Please note that it is often overcrowded in summer. Book your ticket online to save up to 8 euros, and if you visit the park after 6pm, you pay less and the queues are shorter. The park also includes 🐟 *Sea Life Gardaland*, an aquarium with 35 large tanks.

Last, but not least: if you have always wanted to watch rhinos, lions and tigers in the open, drive your car through the 🎭 safari park of *Parco Natura Viva (March–Nov daily, visit their website for varying opening times | 22 euros, children 5-12 years 17 euros | parconaturaviva.it)* 7km inland near Pastrengo. Make sure you keep all windows closed!

WATER SPORTS

Lazise is perfect for those who are looking for fun on holiday. Patrick Planatscher from South Tyrol organises water sports activities such as wakeboarding and flyboarding and fun programmes for children over 5 at *Gardawake (Via Pra del Principe | tel. 34 94 07 60 04 | gardawake.com)*.

WELLNESS

5km south of Lazise in Colà the *Parco Termale del Garda di Villa dei Cedri (Sun-Fri 9.30am-11pm, Sat 9.30am-1pm | 26 euros, after 3pm 20 euros | Piazza di Sopra 4 | villadeicedri.it)* awaits with its warm 37°C thermal lake. It is quieter in the evening when everything is magically illuminated and concerts are held in the park with its ancient trees as well as in the Villa dei Cedri.

INSIDER TIP
Romantic wellness evening

NIGHTLIFE

The evenings in Lazise are a quiet affair. Just sit on the large *Piazza Vittorio Emanuele* and enjoy a glass of wine. The local (surfer) scene enjoys meeting for aperitifs at the *Paparazzi Lounge Cafè (Via Gardesana 52)*.

AROUND LAZISE

🔟 PESCHIERA DEL GARDA
10km south of Lazise / 15 mins by bus route 164

Peschiera is located at the southernmost point of Lake Garda. This is where the water from the lake, fed by the River Sarca in Riva in the north, flows out as the River Mincio in the south towards the Po and ultimately into the Adriatic Sea. The Mincio forms the boundary between the regions of the Veneto and Lombardy. From 1516 onwards, Peschiera came under the rule of Venice and the town was fortified. The impressive and characteristic town walls are a Unesco World Heritage Site. A lot of trains on the Milan–Venice route stop at Peschiera.

The history of fishing on Lake Garda can be traced in the *Museo della Pesca e delle Tradizione Lacustrie (Sat/Sun 10am–12.30pm and 3.30–6.30pm | amicidelgondolin.it)* in the former Habsburg barracks on the left-hand side of the Canale di Mezzo. It includes photographs, fishing equipment and information on the geology of the lake. Great fun for all ages is the ☺ *Latteria Ugolini (Via Fontana 2a | latteriaugolini.com)*: take a cup or cone and create your own ice cream! For decoration, you

INSIDER TIP
Create your own ice cream

can choose between several toppings and sauces. There are no limits to your imagination, and you pay by weight.

A relaxed place by the lake is the *Vecchio Mulino (daily | Strada Bergamini 14 | tel. 04 59 23 30 82 | vecchiomulinobeach.com | €€)*, a beach bar with restaurant (also offering vegan food). Also recommended is the small *Osteria Goto (closed Thu | Piazza Ferdinando di Savoia 2 | tel. 04 59 23 30 14 | €€)* on the edge of the Old Town. The chefs produce excellent pasta dishes. Anyone who fancies a day away from the lake and a gentle bike ride can follow the course of the Mincio from Peschiera to Mantova – which is flat all the way. It's almost 40km along a cycle path. You can take the train back. If you don't have your own bike, you can rent one from *Noleggio Bici (Via Venezia 15 | tel. 34 94 67 80 06 | noleggiobiciclette peschieradelgarda.it)*. A stylish alternative to a bicycle is a Vespa tour! *Motoragazzi (Lungolago Garibaldi 3 | tel. 34 29 28 75 30 | motoragazzi. com)* at the Hotel Acquadolce organize excursions on this iconic scooter around Lake Garda and into the Valpolicella region. ⫘ H8

A sea of flowers and a green oasis: Parco Giardino Sigurtà

13 VALEGGIO & BORGHETTO SUL MINCIO

20km south of Lazise / 30 mins via Peschiera

The culinary speciality of Valeggio (pop. 15,000) are tortellini. Pasta fans can sample them in the excellent restaurants. The pasta is simply sublime at *Alla Borsa (closed Tue/Wed | Via Goito 2 | tel. 04 57 95 00 93 | ristoranteborsa.it | €€–€€€).* If you have trouble deciding what to choose, try the *tris* – a combination of the three most delicious tortellini varieties. Pasta and tortellini, which are incredibly light and delicate, are available to take away at *Pastificio Remelli (Via Alessandro Sala 24 | pastificioremelli.it).*

Passing over the *Ponte Visconteo,* a gigantic stone bridge that was designed as a dam, you get to *Borghetto* which is located on an island in the River Mincio. Here you should visit the popular *Antica Locanda Mincio (closed Wed/Thu | Via Michelangelo Buonarroti 12 | tel. 04 57 95 00 59 | anticalocandamincio.it | €€€).* On the third Tuesday in June the village of Valeggio celebrates its tortellini festival *Festa del Nodo d'Amore* on the bridge across the river on a long table measuring about 600m. It is the "festival of the love knots", as tortellini are called here.

INSIDER TIP
What are "love knots"?

At the northern edge of the town is the large garden and nature park 🐾 *Parco Giardino Sigurtà (2nd half of March and Oct daily 9am–6pm; April–Sept 9am–7pm | 12.50 euros, children 4–14 years 6.50 euros | sigurta.it),* which can be explored on foot, by bicycle or on a miniature train. From mid-March you can admire about one million tulips from 300 different varieties that are on display for the *Tulipanomia,* southern Europe's biggest display of flowering tulips. The park's farm has been converted to a *petting zoo* where children can pet donkeys and sheep.

INSIDER TIP
A sea of tulips

14 FLOWER GARDEN CENTRE & SALEWA OUTLET

11km southeast of Lazise / 15 mins via the SP5

If the weather isn't great, the ▶ *Flover Garden Centre (daily 9am–7.30pm | Via Pastrengo 14–16 | flover.it)* in Bussolengo is a welcome alternative to a walk in the rain. Inspiring exhibitions and workshops on the theme of home and garden are held year-round. And while you are out and about, the 🐗 *Salewa Outlet (Tue-Sat 9am–12.30pm and 3–7.30pm | Via 1° Maggio 26)* in the business park on the SR11 south of the town sells discounted mountain-sport and outdoor clothing.

15 VERONA ☂

1 hr southeast of Lazise by bus route 163 or 164

If you've had enough of the holiday atmosphere and lying on beaches, and fancy a bit of city life, you should head off to Verona (pop. 260,000), just 25km from Lazise. But before you leap in your car, consider taking the train *(trenitalia.com)*. From the south of the lake the train is is easy, and from many other towns on Lake Garda there is a regular bus service to Verona *(atv. verona.it)*. The *Verona Card* (available in museums and tobacco shops, *turismo verona.eu*) is a combined ticket for entrance to museums, churches and major sites of interest as well as for travelling on public transport within the city; a day ticket costs 20 euros.

Due to its position at the end of the route that crosses the Alps via the lowest mountain pass, the Brenner, Verona developed into an important city under the Romans. And its most famous structure dates from Roman times. The Roman amphitheatre ★ *Arena di Verona (Mon 2.30pm–7.30 pm, Tue–Sun 9.30am–7.30pm | on days operas are performed 9am–3.30pm | Piazza Bra | tel. opera festival 04 58 00 51 51 | arena.it)*, dating from the 1st century CE, had its outer walls badly damaged by an earthquake in the 12th century.

WHERE TO START?

Piazza Bra, the large square where the Arena is located, makes the perfect starting point for a tour of the city. It's best to arrive by train as it's only a ten-minute walk from Porta Nuova station to the city centre. If you prefer to travel by car, there is a multi-storey car park on Piazza Citadella, close to the Arena. Please note that vehicle access is restricted in Verona's Old Town. For info about the precise area and times, visit *short.travel/gar28*.

Only four arches of the outer wall are standing today. The arena can be visited during the day, but it is best seen in its full glory on one of its famous opera evenings. Once every month, the 🐦 *Piazza Bra* is the meeting point for romantics and amateur astronomers (for dates visit astrofiliveronesi. it/luna-in-piazza-bra) who gather here on Verona's most beautiful square to view the full moon through telescopes: free for all and extremely romantic!

> INSIDER TIP
> **Full moon in the piazza**

Take Via Roma off the Piazza Bra and treat yourself to an ice cream in Verona's oldest ice cream parlour: *Gelateria Savoia (Via Roma 1b | gelateria savoia.it)*. Some visitors only stop by to admire the 19th-century chandelier made of Murano glass. There are only two of these chandeliers left in the entire world – the other one hangs in the Hermitage in Saint Petersburg.

From the Arena, the Via Roma will take you to the *Castelvecchio (Tue–Sun 8.30am–7.30pm, Mon 1.30–7.30pm | museodicastelvecchio.comune.verona. it)*. The brick-red castle of 1534 is the largest building erected under the Scaligers. Temporary exhibitions are held within its walls. Walking upriver along the upper bank next to the River Adige, you will reach the Piazza Portichetti. This is a slight detour, but it leads to *San Zeno Maggiore* – the church best loved by the locals – with its stunning portal decorated with 48 bronze panels. Detailed information on Verona's churches can be found under *chieseverona.it*.

If you are unable to get opera tickets, you can visit the Arena di Verona during the day

Now take the same route back to the Arena. If you fancy a refreshing drink in the main square, drop in at the Piazza Bra in *Via Mazzini*, Verona's main shopping street. This street leads to the *Piazza delle Erbe*, where a fruit and vegetable market is held every day in the former Roman forum. Our tour continues via the *Piazza dei Signori* and the *Scavi Scaligeri* where photography exhibitions, organised by the Centro Internazionale di Fotografia, are regularly held in the excavated areas. The Scaliger tombs are nearby: above the Gothic graves of the former ruling dynasty are life-sized equestrian statues of family members.

Close by, at *Via Cappello 23*, there is an unremarkable 14th-century house that virtually every visitor to Verona has to have seen – whether or not they have ever read Shakespeare's famous *Romeo and Juliet* or not. *Casa Capuleti* is the official name of Juliet's house *(Mon 1.30–7.30pm, Tue–Sun 8.30am–7.30pm)*. Touching the right-hand breast of the statue of Juliet in the inner courtyard is supposed to make you lucky in love! However, the lovers' balcony – which appears on virtually every postcard of Verona – was only added to the façade in 1940.

The *Osteria Sgarzarie (closed Tue in winter | Corte Sgarzarie 14a | tel. 04 58 00 03 12 | osteriasgarzarie.com | €€)*, not far from Piazza Erbe, is a good place to eat and is far from the madding crowd. Veronese cuisine can be enjoyed in the *Trattoria Tre Marchetti (closed Mon lunchtime and all day Sun; closed Mon only in July/Aug | Vicolo Tre Marchetti 19b | tel. 04 58v 03 04 63 | tremarchetti.it | €€€)*. The restaurant is one of the best the city has to offer and has received numerous awards. ▨ *K8*

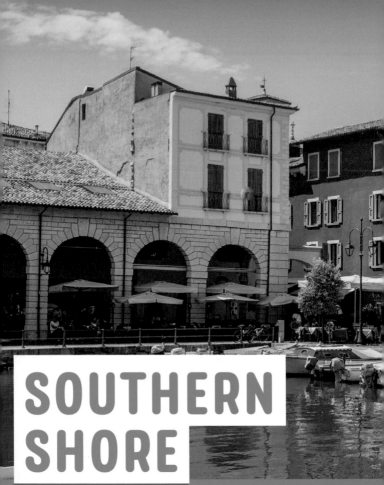

SOUTHERN SHORE

PARTIES & ANTIQUITY

While the northern shore is more dramatic and fjord-like, the southern shore is lovely; it has extensive and pleasant beaches, surrounded by the undulating glacial landscape and vineyards.

The atmosphere in the south is more Mediterranean. Instead of Alpine mountains, the hillsides further inland are more undulating. This is where the famous Lugana white wine is produced.

A picturesque corner of the biggest town on the lake: Porto Vecchio in Desenzano

Sirmione and Desenzano are the main tourist attractions. During the summer months, the historic town of Sirmione is almost overrun with visitors during the day. But in the evenings, when the throngs of day-trippers have departed, it becomes peaceful and pleasant in the maze of lanes. The lively "metropolis" of Desenzano is the biggest town on the lake; it is less affected by crowds, is ideal for shopping and has a lovely jetty in the harbour.

SOUTHERN SHORE

572

Spiaggia dei Canneti

20 mins

11

Desenzano
p.92

Lonato del Garda

567

A4

L O M B A R D I A

Esenta

567

Castiglione delle Stiviere

236

Solferino 1

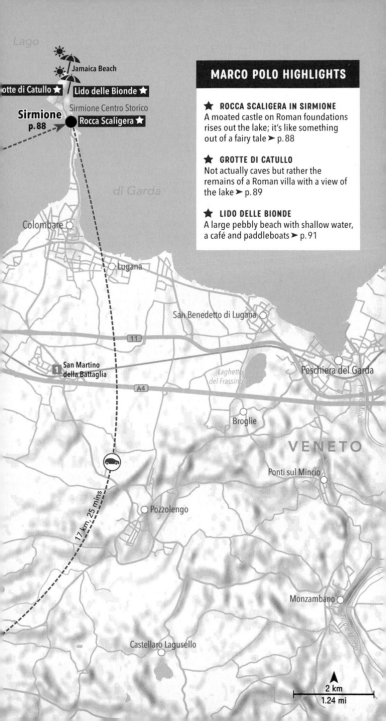

Lago

Jamaica Beach

otte di Catullo ★ | Lido delle Bionde ★

Sirmione
p. 88

Sirmione Centro Storico

Rocca Scaligera ★

di Garda

Colombare ○

○ Lugana

San Benedetto di Lugana ○

(11)

1 | San Martino
della Battaglia

(A4)

Laghetto
del Frassino

Peschiera del Garda

Broglie ○

VENETO

Ponti sul Mincio ○

17 km, 25 mins

○ Pozzolengo

Monzambano ○

Castellaro Lagusello ○

▲
N
2 km
1.24 mi

MARCO POLO HIGHLIGHTS

★ **ROCCA SCALIGERA IN SIRMIONE**
A moated castle on Roman foundations
rises out the lake; it's like something
out of a fairy tale ➤ p. 88

★ **GROTTE DI CATULLO**
Not actually caves but rather the
remains of a Roman villa with a view of
the lake ➤ p. 89

★ **LIDO DELLE BIONDE**
A large pebbly beach with shallow water,
a café and paddleboats ➤ p. 91

SIRMIONE

(▥ G7) **The town (pop. 8,000) has a stunning location: the prominent peninsula juts out right in the middle of the southern shore and points northwards.**

Sirmione is one of the best-known towns on Lake Garda – it's hardly surprising that the pretty streets in the Old Town often get hopelessly crowded. The historic centre beyond the footbridge near the Scaliger Castle can be visited only on foot – and due to the wide canal dug around the

Caves? No. The Grotte di Catullo is actually a Roman villa beside the lake

castle, the Old Town was turned into an island.

Sirmione has not just attracted tourists in modern times. In Roman days its thermal spa was well known. The hot sulphurous spring water, at almost 70°C, emerges from below the bed of the lake, 300m northeast of the 4km-long peninsula.

SIGHTSEEING

ROCCA SCALIGERA ★ ⚑

In the 13th century, Mastino della Scala had a moated castle built inside the protective walls on top of the Roman foundations. Occasionally exhibitions are held in the old fortress grounds at the entrance to the Old Town. But even without any cultural extras the castle has a lot on offer, such as its tower from where there is a wonderful view over the rooftops of the Old Town.

If you fancy some refreshments, for years now, a wonderful old fruit stand has been in place outside the castle, selling pieces of melon and quartered pineapples, slices of lemon and coconut boats. *Tue–Sat 8.30am–7.30pm, Sun 9.15am–5.45pm, Oct–March 8.30am–1.30pm | polomuseale.lombardia.beniculturali.it*

SANT'ANNA

Opposite the castle is this small 14th-century chapel with a 17th-century Baroque interior, where you can admire a Madonna with Child. Sometimes, women who are wishing to have children come here to ask the Madonna for help. *Piazza Castello 1*

SAN PIETRO IN MAVINO
The oldest church in Sirmione stands among the olive trees on a hill above the lake. Built in the eighth century, its interior is decorated with frescos. *Via San Pietro in Mavino*

PARCO TOMELLERI
Those who have had enough of the enoteca, ice cream shops and boutiques in the Old Town can enjoy the wonderful panoramic view of the turquoise lake in this park shaded by olive trees and with white paths through the green grass. This beautiful location is also a popular wedding venue *(sirmionewedding.it). Via Caio Valerio Catullo 7*

GROTTE DI CATULLO ★
Catullus was right: he could hardly have chosen a more beautiful spot on Lake Garda. However, the villa, known as the Grotte di Catullo, was definitely not built by him as he was not wealthy enough.

But what does it matter whether the Roman poet Catullus ever lived on this spot to the south of the lake. It is a delightful location where he probably wrote his eulogy: "O beautiful Sirmione, the gem of all peninsulas and islands." An excursion to this impressive site is more than worthwhile. You can wander through olive groves and look at the extensive remains of the villa walls. The entrance fee includes a visit to the *archaeological museum (Tue–Sat 9am–6pm, Sun 9am–6pm; winter Tue–Sat 8.30am–2pm, Sun 8.30am–5pm).* The clearly labelled displays provide a

good overview of the whole site as well as of the early history of Lake Garda. *Tue–Sat 8.30am–7.30pm; Sun 9.30am–7pm; winter Tue–Sat 8.30am–5pm, Sun 8.30am–2pm | grottedicatullo.beniculturali.it | ⊙ 1¾ hrs*

EATING & DRINKING

IL GIRASOLE
Whether you are looking for pizza, pasta or fish, the "sunflower" has it all. The best tables are on the small outdoor terrace. *Daily | Via Vittorio Emanuele 72 | tel. 0 30 91 91 82 | ilgirasole.info | €–€€*

LA RUCOLA 2.0

A feast for the eyes and taste buds. The romantically lit Rucola will instantly attract you, as will the Michelin-star menu with its intermediate courses and chocolates. Be prepared for the impressive prices ... *Closed Thu | Vicolo Strentelle 3 | tel. 0 30 91 63 26 | ristorantelarucola.it | €€€*

LA SPERANZINA

Here you have the choice between à la carte dishes and a tasting menu. You can enjoy your meal in the peaceful garden with a view of the lake. *April– Oct daily | Via Dante 16 | tel. 03 09 90 62 92 | lasperanzina.it | €€€*

OSTERIA AL TORCOL

This is a wine tavern with a minimal, but authentic menu. The *osteria* has friendly service and an extensive selection of wines mainly from regional producers. *Closed Wed | Via San Salvatore 30 | tel. 03 09 90 46 05 | €€–€€€*

RISORGIMENTO

Extremely friendly staff, excellent food, more than 600 wines stored in the wine "cellar" on the first floor, and all of that in the central Piazza Carducci. What more do you want? *Closed Tue | Piazza Carducci 5 | tel. 0 30 91 63 25 | risorgimento-sirmione.com | €€–€€€*

SHOPPING

The narrow streets of the Old Town on the peninsula are bursting with a huge variety of shops. There is even a patisserie and ice cream parlour for

dogs: *My Dog* in Via Dante sells cupcakes and ice cream for your four-legged friend and arranges for dog sitters. The sulphurous thermal waters of Sirmione are said to help alleviate all kinds of illnesses, including ear, nose and throat issues. It's not surprising that all the pharmacies sell small nasal sprays with "Acqua di Sirmione". Give it a try, it really does help – provided you can put up with a slight smell of rotten eggs …

INSIDER TIP
Healing nasal spray

BEACHES

Several free pebble beaches are located on the southern shore towards

Relaxed shopping: Sirmione's pedestrianised Old Town is ideal for strolling

Peschiera. *Spiaggia Grotte di Catullo* is a tree-lined beach, free of charge, below the excavation site. Unfortunately, it can only be reached by paddle boat or yacht. The ★ ✈ *Lido delle Bionde* is a large flat pebble beach at the northeastern end of the peninsula. There is a café and paddle-boat hire, sun loungers and umbrellas, rather like at a classic Mediterranean resort, complete with a long wooden jetty which doubles as a sunbathing deck and catwalk. At the northernmost end of the peninsula, ✈ *Jamaica Beach* lives up to its name: a flat white shelf that drops into turquoise-blue water and fabulous views. But you can only access it on foot. In the evening, the sun sets behind the mountains on the opposite shore, guaranteeing incredibly romantic holiday photographs. Be careful, though, the flat stones can be slippery!

INSIDER TIP
The perfect sunset beach

WELLNESS

The healing water from Sirmione contains, among other things, salt, iodine and bromide and is used to treat various illnesses. The best place to enjoy the healing springs is *Aquaria (Feb–Dec Sun–Wed 9am–10pm, Thu 11am–midnight, Fri/Sat 9am–midnight; Fri/Sat booking required | Piazza Don A Piatti 1 | termedisirmione. com)*. The vast wellness centre of the thermal baths in Sirmione has several pools, rain-showers and all the accessories required for pure relaxation.

DESENZANO

(□ F7) **Desenzano (pop. 28,000) is the largest – and oldest – town on Lake Garda. When the glaciers that carved out the basin of today's Lake Garda started to retreat northwards at the end of the last Ice Age, this was the first area around the lake that could support life.**

The Romans also settled here as proved by the excavation of a third-century villa with beautiful floor mosaics. Desenzano was repeatedly the object of foreign rulers' desire, as its harbour at the southern end of the lake was a strategically important hub for trade.

What it lacks in the way of beaches it makes up for with its bustling street life. Good shops and window displays can be found in the extensive pedestrian precinct, and you can easily spend hours over a cappuccino or two in one of the cafés on the Piazza Matteotti, just watching the comings and goings. And in the evenings, it's very hard to find room in the bars around the old harbour. While other towns may have nicer lakeside promenades, Desenzano's harbour wall is hard to beat. It comes as no surprise that it is not just the fishermen who can be found here when the sun goes down – this romantic spot is a favourite among couples, too.

On Friday and Saturday evenings, right up until midnight, the narrow pedestrianised streets are completely chock-a-block. Young people from all around meet up here, dressed up to the nines and ready for a night out. After strolling around for a while, they head off to the local clubs.

SIGHTSEEING

LUNGOLAGO CESARE BATTISTI
Walking along the lakeside promenade you have a lovely view across the water – and of the motorboats that sometimes race past at an incredible speed. But they are nothing compared to what Francesco Agello did here back in 1934: he set a new record by reaching a speed of 709kmh! A sculpture in the Mayer & Splendid hotel commemorates this event.

SANTA MARIA MADDALENA
Church lovers will be impressed! The interior dates entirely from the 16th-century Renaissance period and almost resembles an art gallery. *The Last Supper* by Giambattista Tiepolo (1696–1770) is well worth seeing.

VILLA ROMANA
Carpenter Emanuele Zamboni was probably less enthused by history after he discovered the remains of a 100-m^2 Roman yeoman's dwelling when digging the foundations for his house in 1921. The floor mosaics are especially interesting, as is the hypocaust, the Roman equivalent to today's underfloor heating. *Tue–Sun 8.30am–7pm (in winter until 5pm) | Via Crocefisso 22*

CASTELLO

Desenzano castle, originally constructed in the medieval ages, was converted into barracks in the 19th century. It is worth taking a short stroll

uphill to the castle for the far-reaching views of the surrounding countryside – one of the very best along the flat southern shore. *June–Sept Tue–Sun 9.30am–12.30pm and 4.30–7.30pm; April/May and Oct 10am–12.30pm and 3–6pm*

MUSEO CIVICO ARCHEOLOGICO GIOVANNI RAMBOTTI

The museum is housed in a 15th-century cloister – that alone is worth seeing. One of the most interesting exhibits is a 2m-long oak plough dating from the second millennium BCE. *Tue/Wed 9am–1pm, Thu/Fri 3–7pm, Sat/Sun 2.30–7pm | Via Tommaso Dal Molin 7c (in the Chiostro di Santa Maria de Senioribus) | onde.net/desenzano/citta/museo*

EATING & DRINKING

ALLA STELLA

Both tourists and local people love this family-run restaurant in a side street. Whether you order pasta, gnocchi or bread, everything is home-made using organic flour. *Closed Tue lunchtime and Mon | Vicolo Molini 6 | tel. 03 09 91 11 87 | allastella ristorante.it | €€*

A 2,000-year-old stone puzzle: floor mosaic in Desenzano's Roman villa

DESENZANO

KAPPERI

A modern restaurant with a pretty garden and a lively atmosphere. Great food, including a wide selection of gluten-free dishes, and the pizza is available with lactose-free mozzarella. *Closed Mon | Via Nazario Sauro 7 | tel. 03 09 99 18 93 | kapperi.eu | €€-€€€*

RISTORANTE COLOMBA

A bit of retro by the lake: a wonderful spot for a delicious evening meal. Try the wonderfully creamy tiramisu! *Daily | Vicolo dell'Interdetto 16 (Via Porto Vecchio) | tel. 03 09 14 37 01 | ristorantecolomba.it | €-€€€*

BOTTEGA ORAFA MANGANONI

In this fabulous shop, a father with his daughter and son make personalised jewellery to order. *Via Sant'Angela Merici 12 | orafimanganoni.it*

GELATERIA VIVALDI

The ice cream here is the best in town – and only cream and milk from organic farms is used. The pistachio flavour is amazing! *Piazza Matteotti 9 | FB: Gelateria Vivaldi*

HOTEL ALESSI

This hotel owns the elegant and slightly more expensive *Corte Pozzi* in the *palazzo*'s courtyard as well as the cheaper *Trattoria Alessi*, which also has a vegan menu, and the *Wine Bar* with delicious salami and ham platters to go with a glass of wine. *Daily | Via Castello 3 | tel. 03 09 14 17 56 | hotelalessi.com | €-€€*

FRANTOIO DI MONTECROCE

Fresh and (cold) pressed olive oil can be bought at this *azienda agricola* in Montecroce. *Viale Ettore Andreis 84 | frantoiomontecroce.it*

IL LEONE DI LONATO

This shopping centre with 120 shops is 2km from the Desenzano motorway exit in the direction of Castiglione delle Stiviere. *Daily 9am–10pm | illeonedilonato.com*

MARKETS

A *weekly market* is held every Tuesday morning on the road next to the lake and a *farmers' market* is set up every

Thursday morning in Piazza Garibaldi. Every first Sunday of the month – except in January, February and March – the town hosts an *antiques market* in Piazza Malvezzi in the heart of the Old Town, and from May to October a *vintage market* is held every first Saturday of the month *(antiquariato vintagedesenzano.it)*.

SPORT & ACTIVITIES

CYCLING

If you want to explore the hinterland by bicycle, you can follow the six suggestions for tours through the vineyards of the Lugana or the Valtenesi region

(stradadeivini.it). For more tours visit *gardabelloebuono.it/ciclabili*.

HORSE RIDING

In summer in Lonato, lovely 🐎 horse rides (also at night!) for both adults and children from the age of 14 are offered by *Circolo Ippico Spia d'Italia (Via Cerutti 61 | tel. 34 72 58 47 22 | circoloippicospiaditalia.it)*.

SCUBA-DIVING

The southern shore is also great for scuba diving, for example with the instructors at *Tritone Sub (Via Giotto 104 | tel. 32 75 75 17 66 | tritone sub.it)*.

Mercato in Desenzano: a stroll around the market is part of the fun of a great holiday

YOGA

Every Thursday evening at 7pm, from May to September, *Indigo-Yoga (Desenzano Camping Village | Via Vò 4/9 | tel. 33 98 25 02 59 | indigoyoga. eu)* offers a Hatha yoga session. On Mondays at 7pm you can test your sense of balance and practise yoga on a stand-up paddleboard.

INSIDER TIP
Yoga on the water

BEACHES

Desenzano and the surrounding area have a wide selection of beaches: to the north of the harbour is the pebble beach of *Spiaggia Feltrinelli* with sun loungers and parasols. The nudist beach of *Spiaggia dei Canneti*, 1km further north at Punta Vò, has been a meeting place of the local gay scene for decades. In the other direction, in Rivoltella, trendy young people congregate on *Spiaggia d'Oro* for bathing and celebrating at the *Golden Beach Club (goldenbeach. playfun.tv).* Desenzano and the Sirmione peninsula, as well as to the north along the hilly Valtenesi, you will come across a number of other places to swim or sunbathe.

WELLNESS

If you book in advance, the (expensive) spa including sauna, Turkish bath and a small pool in the *Hotel Mayer & Splendid* in the Old Town is also open to non-residents. *Daily 11am–9pm | Sun–Fri 65 euros/person, for 2 people 37 euros/person; Sat 90/45 euros |* Piazza Papa 10 | tel. 03 09 14 22 53 | hotelmayerdesenzano.com*

For those who enjoy a bit of Saturday-night fever there's no avoiding Desenzano – the town is *the* nightlife centre on the lake.

ART CLUB

Despite its location outside town, this nightclub is always packed. Locals and tourists of all ages come here to dance to the beats of varying DJs every Wednesday, Friday and Saturday. Drag queen Madame Sisì and her troupe also entertain the audience with fantastic shows. A brilliant atmosphere! *Wed, Fri and Sat from 11.30pm | Via Mella 4 | artclubdisco.com*

COCO BEACH CLUB

For a bit of Miami flair on Lake Garda, locals and tourists alike flock to the fine sandy beach at the Lido di Lonato to party the night away in style. *Wed and Fri–Sun from 6pm | Via Catullo 5 | cocobeachclub.com*

AROUND DESENZANO

■ SOLFERINO & SAN MARTINO DELLA BATTAGLIA

15km to Solferino south of Desenzano / 20 mins via the SP567 and Castel Venzago

The area around Lake Garda was

The remains of war: skulls in San Pietro in Solferino

frequently the scene of fierce battles in the fight for the unification of Italy by the Italian *Risorgimento*. Among the bloodiest were the Battle of San Martino della Battaglia and the Battle of Solferino, a few miles to the south. In 1859, the *Risorgimento* defeated the Austrian army under Emperor Franz Joseph. The foundations for a united Italy were laid, and included: the Venetian Republic annexed from Austria, Piedmont ruled by the House of Savoy, the Kingdom of Sicily and papal Rome. It was achieved at the cost of 25,000 lives.

Tens of thousands of wounded were left to their own fate on the battlefields. This made the name Solferino known throughout the world. Henri Dunant, an extremely rich Swiss man, was so shocked at the sight of these helpless soldiers that he founded the Red Cross – originally a charitable organisation set up to aid the wounded. Seven thousand skulls have been preserved in the church of *San Pietro* in Solferino as a reminder of the atrocities of war.

San Martino also has a tower, the *Torre di San Martino*, erected as a monument and 74m high. Inside, a series of frescoes relates the history of the *Risorgimento*. A 👪 child-friendly, 21-km circular *cycle path (short.travel/ gar26)* leads from Desenzano railway station to the memorial tower. *solferinoesanmartino.it* ⬚ *G8*

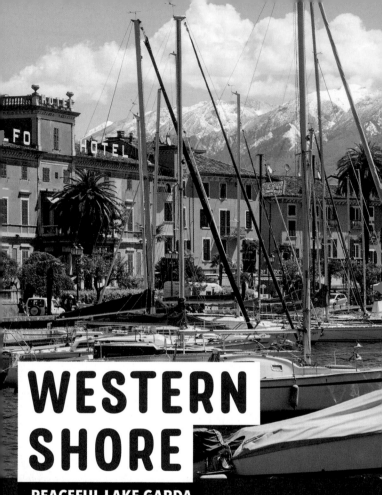

WESTERN SHORE

PEACEFUL LAKE GARDA

And how did it all begin? In 1880, the Austrian Louis Wimmer travelled down the western side of the lake and recognised how much it would appeal to his fellow countrymen. He began by building the Grand Hotel Gardone and, in doing so, set the ball rolling for tourism on Lake Garda.

In the early 20th century, ever more luxury hotels went up and, instead of lemon trees, vineyards and olive groves, beautiful parks were laid out, whose lovely trees still give this region its special

Maritime still life: boats moored by the promenade in Maderno

charm. In 1921, the Italian poet Gabriele D'Annunzio, an eccentric and a dandy, came to live here. His house, Vittoriale degli Italiani, is now a museum and still retains the spirit of that time.

At the southern end of the western shore the mountains take a step back from the lake. The lakeside road winds its way elegantly along the shoreline or else turns inland. The lake at this point is so wide it can seem like the open sea when the weather is hazy. Visiting foodies will be treated to the best fine dining to be had on the lake.

Baitoni

9 Lago d'Idro

Vesta

Anfo

Forno d'Ono

Lavenone

Pertica Alta

Capov

34 km, 50 mins

Idro

33 km, 45 m

237

Vestone

Treviso Bresciano

Nozza

17 km, 25 m

Casto

Barnico

Barghe

Bione

Preseglie

San Faustino

Sabbio Chiese

Carpeneda

Agnosine

Odolo

Vobarno

LOMBARDIA

10 km, 15 mins

Roè

San Mic

Caino

Volciano

Gazzino

Vallio Terme

Bondone

Lungolago di Salò ★

Salò
p. 102

Villa di Salò

Porte

Gavardo

Soprazocco

San Felice del Benaco

Serle

Puegnago
sul Garda

Paitone

Muscoline

18 km, 30 mi

4 Franciacorta
Outlet Village

Nuvolento

Prevalle

Polpenazze del Garda

So

Botticino Mattina

Calvagese della Riviera

Moniga
del Garda

Botticino Sera

Soiano del Lago

Mazzano

Rezzato

Padenghe sul Garda

Lido di Padeng

Molinetto

Bedizzole

Ciliverghe

3 km
1.86 mi

A4

11

Magasa · Cadria
Tremosine

8 **Strada della Forra** ★
Terrazza del Brivido ★

Cadria
Turano
Moerna
ollone
Costa

Campione del Garda

Madonna di Montecastello **7**
Tignale

Pieve
Malcesine

Cassone

Assenza

9 **Lago di Valvestino**

Muslone

Porto

Marniga

Parco Fontanella ★
Gargnano
p. 113

Castelletto

Navazzo

Prada

29

45
249
VENETO

Lago

Gaino

Pai di Sotto

Toscolano-
·Maderno
6 **Toscolano-Maderno**

Gardone Riviera p. 107
Giardino Botanico André Heller ★
Vittoriale degli Italiani ★

Torri del
Benaco

1 **Isola del Garda**

3 **Manerba del Garda**

di Garda

Sirmione

MARCO POLO HIGHLIGHTS

★ **LUNGOLAGO DI SALÒ**
Join locals and visitors for a stroll along
the prom – it's the longest on the lake
➤ p.102

★ **GIARDINO BOTANICO ANDRÉ HELLER**
André Heller's dream garden, where
modern sculptures are hidden in a
magical park in Gardone Sopra ➤ p.108

★ **VITTORIALE DEGLI ITALIANI**
Gabriele D'Annunzio's bizarre residence
➤ p.109

★ **PARCO FONTANELLA**
One of the largest free beaches on the
western shore ➤ p.115

★ **TERRAZZA DEL BRIVIDO**
Restaurant terraces that jut out a long
way above the lake ➤ p.116

★ **STRADA DELLA FORRA**
This panoramic road winds up to Pieve
from the western shore ➤ p.116

SALÒ

(*F6*) **Salò (pop. 11,000) has had the longest ★ promenade on Lake Garda for more than 120 years – the Lungolago was built after an earthquake in 1901.**

In 2004 there was another earthquake which badly damaged a number of buildings. However, the lakeside promenade has since been widened and extended. It now runs for almost 3km right round to the cemetery with its eye-catching cypresses on the other side of the bay. It is virtually car-free, with one café after another,

Elegant Salò is protected in a bay

and benches lining the shore. The little fishing boats bobbing about in the water are taken out into the lake in the mornings in search of what Salò's gourmet restaurants will later serve their guests: *lavarello* and *corregone* – Lake Garda whitefish. The town nestles in a bay at the southern end of the western shore and, even if today it is a busy little place, the former spa town still exudes a certain elegance.

Salò has always been wealthier than the neighbouring fishing villages. In 1377 it was declared the administrative centre for the western shore by the ruling Visconti of Milan. And in 1426 the Venetians named it the "Magnifica Patria della Riviera". Towards the end of the more recent period under Fascist rule, Mussolini raised Salò to the capital of the Fascist Socialist Republic.

SIGHTSEEING

PALAZZO DEL PODESTÀ

In the 16th century the old 14th-century Town Hall was given a Venetian façade with an arcade, and it suits the building very well. However, nothing of the original remains – the earthquake in 1901 also destroyed the Palazzo del Podestà.

SANTA MARIA ANNUNZIATA

Salò is the only place on Lake Garda with a cathedral. Work started on the late Gothic building in 1453. A white Renaissance portal was later added to the plain brick façade. *Daily 8.30am–noon and 3.30–7pm | Piazza Duomo | parrocchiadisalo.it*

HOTEL LAURIN

The Laurin is the most beautiful Art Deco building on the lake. It is now an elegant hotel. If you only want a drink you can go into the lobby and marvel at the exquisite interior at your leisure. During the Fascist dictatorship, the building housed the Foreign Ministry for a time as well as Mussolini himself. *Viale Landi 9 | hotellaurinsalo.com*

EATING & DRINKING

LA CAMPAGNOLA

Angelo Dal Bon's restaurant is one of the best in the area; his cuisine follows the "slow food" principle. One gourmet speciality is the salt-coated entrecôte steak. The food leaves as little to be desired as the unbeatable extensive wine list. *Closed Sun evening, all day Monday and Tue lunchtime | Via Brunati 11 | tel. 0 36 52 21 53 | lacampagnola1952.it | €€€*

LA CASA DEL DOLCE

This is where you'll find the creamiest chocolate ice cream anywhere on the lake. You can watch it being made in the parlour next door. *Piazza Duomo 1*

PASTICCERIA VASSALLI

Tasty sandwiches are on offer here as well as cakes and *bacetti di Salò* – "kisses from Salò" – delicious nut praliné chocolates. *Closed Tue in winter | Via San Carlo 84–86 | pasticceriavassalli.com*

TRATTORIA ALLE ROSE

Gianni Briarava serves only the very best in his contemporary-style

Music and chocolate at Pasticceria Vassalli

restaurant. The classic *cucina gardesana* has been blended with new ideas ranging from juniper-smoked stag tartar and pike mousse-filled ravioli to elegant fish and meat dishes. *Closed Wed | Via Gasparo da Salò 33 | tel. 0 36 54 32 20 | trattoriaallerose.it | €€-€€€*

SHOPPING

The Old Town of Salò is great for shopping. Most of the shops are in

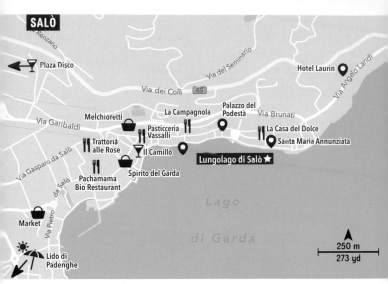

Via San Carlo that runs parallel to and slightly set back from the shore.

MARKET

Every Saturday morning, south of the Old Town. This is one of the biggest markets on the lake.

MELCHIORETTI

This grocery shop looks like a chemist's – and that's exactly what it used to be. Built in 1805, it has remained virtually unchanged since 1870 – except that instead of bars of soap you'll now find pesto and pasta. *Piazza Zanelli 11*

SPIRITO DEL GARDA

This shop is the adult equivalent to a children's sweets shop: wine, liquors, olive oil, vinegar and pickled produce … simply wonderful! *Piazza Bresciani 3 | spiritodelgarda.it*

SPORT & ACTIVITIES

ADVENTURE PARK

Those looking for adventure can climb swaying rope bridges and shaky tree trunks at 🎪 *Parco Avventura Rimbalzello (June–Aug daily 10am–8pm; April/May and Sept/Oct Sat 2–7pm, Sun 10am–7pm | 19–24 euros, children 3–6 years 10 euros, under 15 years 18–21 euros | rimbalzelloadventure.com)*, about 1km northeast of Salò in *Barbarano*.

CYCLING & JOGGING

One of the most beautiful places to jog on Lake Garda is the route around the traffic-free bay of Salò. The best time is in the morning when relatively few people are out and about. There are also many cycle paths around Salò, including one that leads to Lonato near Desenzano.

BEACHES

When the Lungolago was extended, two small beaches were created opposite the bay, not far from the cemetery. They are easy to spot thanks to the distinctive row of cypresses. Close by is the Valtenesi – a hilly area around Manerba. Here, you will find a number of other places to swim: *Porto San Felice* has a flat pebble beach; dogs are not allowed on the *Spiaggia La Romantica* in Manerba which also has a restaurant. In the evenings, there is live music on the free-of-charge beach of *Baia Bianca (baiabianca.it)*. You can wade through the shallow water to the isle of *San Biagio*, which is beautiful but you do have to pay a fee because it belongs to a campsite. In *Moniga del Garda* there are pebble and rocky beaches that are free of charge. Even further south, at Padenghe, is the ✻ *Lido di Padenghe*, a particularly beautiful pebble beach with parasol hire.

NIGHTLIFE

The whole length of the Lungolago in Salò is given over to strolling in the evening. Just drift along, back and forth. Especially in summer, young people meet in *Piazza Vittorio Emanuele II*, known locally as "Fossa". After a recent restructuring, the square is now mainly pedestrianised.

IL CAMILLO

Delicious *aperitivi* and cocktails, small bites to eat and various events are the features of this nice bar – plus the particularly friendly staff! *Closed Mon.* | *Piazza Cavour 23/25* | *FB: Il Camillo*

PLAZA DISCO

Things don't really get going at this disco in the western suburbs until around midnight. Hits and beats for all ages are played in the three different rooms. *Via Domenico Signori 41* | *Roè Volciano* | *plazadisco.it*

AROUND SALÒ

1 ISOLA DEL GARDA

15 mins by boat from Salò

The larger island in the lake with its magnificent villa and wonderfully manicured park is privately owned but can be visited during the summer months from various places on the lake as part of organized 👥 *tours (31 euros, children 18 euros).* Tours from Salò start on Sundays at 10am. *Booking required: tel. 32 86 12 69 43* | *isoladelgarda.com* ⊞ *G6*

2 SAN FELICE DEL BENACO

7km southeast of Salò / 15 mins via the shoreline road

Most campsites on Lake Garda are to be found between Salò and Desenzano; hotels are noticeably fewer in number here. The beaches tend to be pretty full, particularly at weekends; although access to most of the beaches not owned by the campsites is free of charge, the car parks are

Explore the ruins and enjoy the views: excursion to Rocca di Manerba

not. But away from the lake you can wind your way between vineyards and olive groves. The centre of San Felice (pop. 3,400) and its churches are worth a detour. There is a small beach near Porto Portese for swimming.

Home-made pasta and a massive serving of fish starters are available in Porto Portese at the *Ristorante Osvaldo* (*daily | Piazzale Marinai d'Italia 5 | tel. 0 3656 21 08 | €€*). Good olive oil can be found at *Frantoio Cooperativa Agricola San Felice del Benaco* (*Via delle Gere 2 | oliofelice.com*). ⌑ F6

■ MANERBA DEL GARDA

12km southeast of Salò / 20 mins via the SP572

This little town (pop. 5,000) is known for its picturesque shoreline with the small harbour of Porto Dusano and long beaches. From *Rocca di Manerba*, the castle ruins atop a striking cliff near Montinelle, you can enjoy a wonderful view of the southern side of the lake. The ruins are part of the Rocca di Manerba Natural Archaeological Park. To make it easier for visitors to explore this area with its rich history, an innovative

oil mill invites you to an aperitif *(5 euros)*: after a guided tour, visitors can taste the olive oil and other native products. 🐷 And if you reserve a table for dinner at the restaurant *(€€-€€€)*, you get the aperitif for free. *⊞ F6*

4 FRANCIACORTA OUTLET VILLAGE

55km west of Salò / 40-50 mins via the A4 to exit Ospitaletto

Two hundred shops offering reductions of up to 70 % on brand products: this shopping mile by the A4 just after Brescia can be reached from Salò in about 40 minutes. *Daily 10am-8pm | motorway exit Ospitaletto | franciacortaoutlet.it. ⊞ B-C6*

GARDONE RIVIERA

(⊞ F-G 5-6) **If you want to time-travel and feel like the very first tourists on Lake Garda, Gardone Riviera is the place to go.**

The gardens, along with the stately villas and old hotels along the shoreline, are testimony to Gardone's glorious past. Around 1880, Austrian engineer Louis Wimmer came to Gardone, fell in love with the landscape and built the pompous Grand Hotel Gardone Riviera.

The best things about Gardone are its parks and gardens. Taking the steep roads and paths that lead up from the shore, you will find yourself walking in the shade of old cypress

bike-sharing system, Manerba in Bici, has been set up. For information, contact *Manerba Servizi Turistici | Via Zanardelli 17 | tel. 03 65 55 27 45 | manerbaserviziuristici.it.*

Surrounded by olive trees on the outskirts of Manerba lies the *Azienda Agricola Manestrini (Soiano del Lago | Via Avanzi 11 | tel. 03 65 50 22 31 | manestrini.it).* The complex consists of an oil mill, a fine restaurant with a view of the lake and holiday flats. Every Tuesday evening at 5.30pm, the trees and magnolias. The town is protected by hills and mountains so that Mediterranean plants do well here. A stay in Lungolago D'Annunzio can work wonders: here you can easily forget that the village is not even on the lakeside but above it. Gardone Sopra, with its houses all huddled around San Nicola's parish church, now has a population of 2,700 and is a little sidelined these days. A narrow path with a magnificent view of the lake winds its way between the houses. And everyone heads for the attraction *par excellence*, Vittoriale degli Italiani, the poet Gabriele D'Annunzio's eccentric retirement home.

INSIDER TIP
Panoramic walk high above the lake

SIGHTSEEING

GIARDINO BOTANICO ANDRÉ HELLER ★

Originally this botanic garden in Gardone Sopra was just one of the many wonderful parks in the area. But since the Austrian artist and performer André Heller bought it at the end of the 1980s, it has become more than just that. Splashing fountains can be found among huge trees, and you might spot a modern sculpture by Keith Haring or Mimmo Paladino hidden in a glade. André Heller enthuses about his collection of flora from different places from around the world, a paradise that he never ceases to wonder at: "Edelweiss in the middle of orchid meadows, tree ferns several

A magical composition of nature, art and water was created in Gardone by André Heller

feet high next to magnificent pomegranates. Streams and waterfalls with sacred koi carp, trout and reflections made by dragonflies, hills of dolomite rock next to cacti and towering ivies." *Daily March–Oct 9am–7pm | Via Roma 2 | hellergarden.com | ⏲ 1 hr*

VITTORIALE DEGLI ITALIANI ★
Are you fascinated by the life of one of the most enigmatic personalities of Italian history? Then visit the "victory monument of the Italians". The war hero, philosopher, poet, Fascist and maverick, Gabriele D'Annunzio (1863–1938), not only built a house here in 1921, but also an almost inaccessible and bizarre collection of buildings. The attractions, which are worth seeing in addition to the poet's house, include a *war museum* with the legendary plane from which D'Annunzio dropped leaflets over Vienna during World War One, a warship, the mausoleum as well as Isotta Fraschini vintage car and old Fiat T4. In the open-air theatre, cultural events are regularly performed during the summer *(anfiteatrodelvittoriale.it)*. In *Vittoriale park* visitors are free to roam, whereas guided tours are obligatory in the *house*. As admission tickets are limited, it is best to purchase them beforehand online. *Daily 9am–5pm, April–Oct until 8pm, museum and house Nov–March closed Mon | vittoriale.it | ⏲ 3–3½ hrs for the entire complex*

The Vittoriale: a bizarre collection of curiosities by poet D'Annunzio

MUSEO IL DIVINO INFANTE
The world's first (and supposedly only) museum of the Christ Child: the 200 sculptures that make up this collection date from a period of three centuries and are truly unique. *Easter–Sept Fri–Sun 3–7pm, mid-Nov–mid-Jan Tue–Sun 2–6pm (Dec 20–Jan 6 daily 10am–6pm) | Via dei Colli 34 | il-bambino-gesu.com*

EATING & DRINKING

AGLI ANGELI
Patrizia and Elisabetta Pellegrini's cooking in Gardone Sopra is

becoming more and more elegant and refined. Booking essential! *Closed Tue | Via Dosso 7 | tel. 0 36 52 09 91 | agliangeli.biz | €€–€€€*

ANTICO BROLO

Delectable and creative traditional fare is served right in the town centre. Chefs Enrico and Marcello are very attentive and do their best to ensure for a pleasant dining experience. *Closed Tue lunchtime and Mon | Via Carere 10 | tel. 0 36 52 14 21 | ristoranteanticobrolo.it | €€–€€€*

LIDO 84

The view of the lake doesn't get more spectacular – and the food lives up to expectations: the restaurant has a Michelin star and offers the surprising combination of typical ingredients from the Lombardy region with exotic spices. *Closed Tue/Wed | Corso Zanardelli 196 | tel. 0 36 52 00 19 | ristorantelido84.com | €€€*

RISTORANTE PIZZERIA NABLUS

Local people love the delicious pizzas, and the wonderful sea views are free of charge! *Closed Tue | Via Supiane 1 | tel. 0 36 54 36 71 | ristorantenablus. com | €€*

SHOPPING

LABORATORIO ARTIGIANALE KARIN STEINBACHER

Karin from Germany is one of the many expats in Gardone. In her small idyllic shop she sells home-made jams from citrus fruits, *mostarda* (mustard fruits) and limoncello

– according to many locals probably the best on Lake Garda! *Daily 10am–3pm, in winter until 1pm | Via Caduti 23*

INSIDER TIP
Lake Garda limoncello

VINTAGE MARKET

A small flea market is held along the promenade once a month where you can find antiques and objects from the 1960s and 1970s. The dates vary.

SPORT & ACTIVITIES

At *Big Sur Sky Park (Via Val di Sur | tel. 34 72 28 43 61 | gardabigsur.com)* in San Michele, those who dare can undertake a tandem paragliding adventure.

BEACHES

Spiaggia Rimbalzello to the south of the town costs 6.50 euros (12.50 euros incl. parasol and sun lounger). Free beaches are near the Villa delle Rose in Fasano and another, very small one can be found near the casino on Via Zanardelli.

NIGHTLIFE

Gardone is better known for its culture than its nightlife. ✈ Live music can be enjoyed free of charge along the lake promenade on alternate evenings; in the Vittoriale there are theatre performances and concerts *(anfi teatrodelvittoriale.it)*. One of the more stylish places to go on the lake is the former lighthouse *Torre San Marco (Tue–Sun 10.30pm–3am | Via*

As the name suggests, the trattoria Agli Angeli serves heavenly food

Zanardelli 132 | torresanmarco.it) with its piano bar and club. The fairy-tale tower was once owned by poet Gabriele D'Annunzio. *Caffè Wimmer (Piazza Wimmer 5)* or *Bar Le Rose (Via dei Caduti 19)* in Gardone Sopra are also nice.

AROUND GARDONE

⑤ SAN MICHELE
Approx. 3km north of Gardone / 1 hr via the signposted hiking trail
If you like, you can take the hour-long walk up to the village of San Michele. The path (waymarked from Vittoriale) misses out all the twists and turns of the road. At the top, hearty traditional

dishes and delicious tiramisu await at *Miramonti (closed Mon in winter | Via Panoramica 96 | tel. 0 36 52 09 05 | hrmiramonti.it | €).* Make a reservation on Sundays! *F5*

⑥ TOSCOLANO-MADERNO
5km northeast of Gardone / 10 mins via the Gardesana Occidentale
The twin community (pop. 8,000) lies slightly to the north, where the Toscolano stream feeds into the lake. Its upper reaches are the *Valle delle Cartiere*, the "paper factory valley", which is well worth a visit. Back in the 14th century, the paper mills were already selling their wares throughout Europe, and later even in the Orient. A path passes by the ruins. It's best to start from the Gardesana by the turn to Gaino. On the path you'll see two mill-stones. These were used to turn rags

Have a look in passing at the Baroque garden of Villa Bettoni-Cazzago

into pulp for the production of paper. After about 30 mins you will reach the well-presented *Museo della Carta (April–June and Sept daily 10am–6pm; July/Aug 10am–7pm; Oct Sat/Sun 10am–5pm | valledellecartiere.it).*

Sant'Andrea Apostolo church in Maderno is worth seeing. You may not notice it at first as the more recent parish church opposite dominates the scene. But the 12th-century Romanesque chapel with its façade of pink, grey and white stripes is more interesting. Look for the details in the porch (fruit, leaf tendrils, plaited ornamentation): the skill of the masons almost a millennium ago is

astounding. The harmonious interior is dominated by heavy pillars and columns with their imposing capitals. Older still by another thousand years is the Roman *Villa Nonii Arrii* in Toscolano *(May–Oct Sat/Sun 10am–noon and 3–6pm | Piazza Santissima Maria del Benaco)* with its well-preserved mosaic pavements.

The *Osteria del Boccondivino (closed lunchtimes and Tue | Via Cavour 71 | tel. 03 65 64 25 12 | €€)* in Maderno specialises in fish. In the *Osteria Gatto d'Oro (closed Tue | Via Fratelli Bianchi 41 | tel. 03 65 54 09 75 | FB: L'Osteria Gatto d'Oro | €€),* owner Sabina lovingly looks after her guests. You may feel as if you are in a bric-a-brac shop (there are cat statues and images everywhere, and four-legged friends are always welcome), but the food is delicious. *G5*

GARGNANO

(*G5*) **The name Gargnano (pop. 2,900) actually applies to three little villages, each with a harbour and each as lovely as the other two. The villages are linked by the Gardesana road: first of all, you will come to the largest of the three, Gargnano itself, with its short lakeside promenade, followed by Villa and then Bogliaco. Each of the three has just one one-way road leading into the village.**

Before the Gardesana was built in the 1930s, the most common way of getting about was by boat. Hiking and strolling, swimming and dining – these are the reasons for coming here. And in the evening the pace is just as slow. Gargnano got out of step once for a short time: during the Fascist period of the "Republic of Salò" near the end of World War II, dictator Benito Mussolini had his official residence here in the Villa Feltrinelli.

SIGHTSEEING

PALAZZO FELTRINELLI

The *palazzo* was requisitioned by the Fascist government in the 1940s and was used as the general headquarters of Benito Mussolini. Today, the University of Milan holds a summer school here with Italian language courses *(unimi.it)* for students from around the world.

INSIDER TIP
Learn Italian in the palazzo

VILLA BETTONI-CAZZAGO

A magnificent building! The special thing about the privately owned villa in the district of Bogliaco is the architectural consistency that harmoniously defines the villa as well as its perfectly landscaped garden that is usually open in April for a garden show.

MARINA DI BOGLIACO

The harbour in Bogliaco is elegant and exclusive and surrounded by only a few houses. In this small community you can admire the sleek yachts and smart sailing boats – especially in September when the biggest sailing regatta on Lake Garda is held here and several hundred participants and sailing enthusiasts gather.

EATING & DRINKING

Fewer than 3,000 residents, but three Michelin-star restaurants: Gargnano is gourmet heaven. *Villa Feltrinelli (villafeltrinelli.com)*, not to be confused with the *palazzo* of the same name, would be worth visiting for its beautiful location alone because it is arguably the most romantic villa on the lake! Chef Stefano Baiocco has been awarded two Michelin stars. His speciality is a salad with 25 different edible flowers! Family-run *Tortuga* restaurant *(ristorantelatortuga.it)* has had a Michelin star since 1980, and in 2018 the *Villa Giulia* restaurant *(villa giulia.it)* also received a star. But don't worry, Gargnano has alternatives for those who can't or don't want to spend so much money on food:

ALLO SCOGLIO

Here you can eat in a pretty garden on the lakeside in Bogliaco. The building is a former gatehouse to the Villa Bettoni-Cazzago. Fish is a speciality here. *Closed Mon | Via Barbacane 2 | tel. 0 36 57 10 30 | alloscoglio.it | €€*

RISTORANTE FORNICO

Are you looking for a rustic dining experience? Every Sunday, Marco grills meat kebabs and serves them with polenta – a popular dish with the locals. On any day, the cuisine is traditional and delicious. *Closed Mon and Tue evenings | Via Sole 13 | tel. 0 36 57 10 58 | ristorantefornico.it | €–€€*

TRATTORIA SAN MARTINO

Fine cuisine using local produce. The *spaghetti alla carbonara di lago* with smoked Lake Garda tench is truly delicious and the terrace is quite romantic. *Closed Mon | Via Roma 33 | tel. 0 36 57 14 36 | trattoriasanmartino.it | €€*

SPORT & ACTIVITIES

SAILING & WINDSURFING

At the northern edge of town, by Fontanella Beach, is the *OK-Surf (tel. 32 84 71 77 77 | oksurf.it)* surf school.

Is there still room in the budget for a drink on the terrace after a wellness day at the Lefay?

Sailing courses for adults and children are organised by *Circolo Vela (Via Conte Bettoni 23 | tel. 0 36 57 14 33 | centomiglia.it)* in Bogliaco.

TENNIS

Bogliaco has two *tennis courts (tel. 36 63 40 24 23 | tennisbogliaco.it)* where you can play during the day and in the evening as well.

BEACHES

Entry to the ★ ☆ *Parco Fontanella*, to the north of the villages, is free of charge and there's a beach. Here you can lie in the shade of olive trees; there is table tennis, a bar and a big car park (parking fee). Bogliaco has the beautiful sandy beach of *Spiaggia Corno* (entry is free of charge). The small pebble beach *Spiaggia della Gial* on Via Rimembranze also welcomes dogs.

WELLNESS

LEFAY RESORT

In the grandiose five-star complex high above the lake you can swim in the infinity pool while looking straight at Lake Garda – the pool literally merges with the horizon and is superbly suited for Instagram posts – or relax in the extensive spa and wellness area. You will feel much lighter afterwards – as will your wallet. A day including a 50-minute massage costs 140 euros, from Friday to Sunday 170 euros. *Via Angelo Feltrinelli 118 | tel. 03 65 24 18 00 | lefayresorts.com*

NIGHTLIFE

The pace in Gargnano is leisurely – which is precisely why regular visitors love this resort. After dinner, you can treat yourself to an ice cream on the lakeside. The biggest and best are served in the *Bar Azzurra (Piazza Angelo Feltrinelli 11)*.

AROUND GARGNANO

7 MADONNA DI MONTECASTELLO

13km northeast of Gargnano / 25 mins via the Gardesana Occidentale and SP38

This hermitage, at an altitude of 700m, is a popular place for day-trippers and pilgrims alike, with a wonderful view of Lake Garda and the mountains. *Daily Easter–Oct 9am–6pm | santuario montecastello.it ⊞ H4*

8 TREMOSINE

18km to Pieve northeast of Gargnano / 30 mins via the Gardesana Occidentale

Aromatic Alpine cheese, untouched nature and amazing views make the quiet plateau in the municipality of Tremosine a paradise for food connoisseurs, nature lovers and sports fans. All of the eighteen villages – apart from Campione with its harbour – are nestled between the steep rock canyons and lush meadows of the Alto Garda Bresciano National Park high

above the lake. Local specialities such as cheese, salami and sausages can be purchased from the *agriturismo*  *Alpe del Garda (daily | Via Provinciale 1 | located in Polzone | tel. 03 65 95 30 50 | alpedelgarda.it | €)* with its show dairy, farm shop and playground.

The main centre, *Pieve*, is high above the lake. Visitors are attracted by the ★ *Terrazza del Brivido* at the *Hotel Paradiso (Viale Europa 1 | terrazzadelbrivido.i)*: a terrace that juts out frighteningly far over the lake below. Meanwhile, near the terrace of hotel *Miralago (Piazza Cozzaglio 2 | miralago. it)*, is a narrow path that takes you down the seemingly vertical cliff face. This path, the *Sentiero del*

INSIDER TIP
Hiking with a head for heights

Porto, is marked as Route 201 and was once the only way down to the lake.

Today, the breathtaking ★ *Strada della Forra* (see p. 127), which was built in 1913 through the narrow gorge of the Brasa torrent, also takes you to the town. This road is where Daniel Craig sped during a hair-raising escape in the James Bond film *Quantum of Solace*. In real life, speeding is not advised: the road is narrow, regulated with traffic lights and a challenge even for experienced drivers.

Outdoor enthusiasts can head to *SKYclimber (Via Dalco 3 | tel. 3 35 29 32 37 | skyclimber.it)*, who can organise canyoning trips, a mountain-bike training circuit and guided rope-climbing tours. There are also many options for children. *H3–4*

Lake-hopping around Gargnano: Lago d'Idro

9 LAGO D'IDRO & LAGO DI VALVESTINO

37km to Lake Idro northwest of Gargnano / 1 hr via the SP9 and SP58

A curvy little road leads from Gargnano to *Lago di Valvestino* through the surprisingly untouched countryside that has yet to see much tourist traffic. With its crystal-clear water, this reservoir has a wild kind of beauty. The Toscolano stream, which powers the paper mills in Toscolano-Maderno, is dammed by the lake. On certain dates from May to September, you can visit the *Osservatorio Astronomico di Cima Rest (booking at Infopoint Valvestino | tel. 03 65 74 50 60 | visitvalvestino.it)*, located at the tip of the lake on the Cima Rest plateau, which you access via the village of Magasa.

INSIDER TIP
Reach for the stars

From the Valestino valley, a serpentine road runs through the village of Capovalle and steeply back down to the shimmering water of *Lake Idro*. The whole region has a certain mountainous Tyrolean feel but the villages are Italian with their narrow streets and Romanesque churches. In *Pieve Vecchia*, at the south end of the lake, you can stop for a break in one of the street cafés and watch the motorbikes pass or you can head for the *Pizzeria Milano (closed Tue | Via Trento 35 | tel.03 65 82 33 91 | hotelmilano.bs.it | €)* for a bite to eat. *F–G 3–4*

DISCOVERY TOURS

Want to get under the skin of the region? Then our discovery tours are the ideal guide – they provide advice on which sights to visit, tips on where to stop for that perfect holiday snap, a choice of the best places to eat and drink, and suggestions for fun activities.

❶ THE PEAKS OF MONTE BALDO

➤ Enjoy 360-degree views from the cable car
➤ Admire marmots (with a bit of luck …)
➤ Smell the fresh mountain air at 2,000m

📍	Monte Baldo cable car top station	🏁	Monte Baldo cable car top station
⇄	3km	🚶	5–6 hrs (3½ hrs total walking time)
📶	medium	↗	440m

ℹ️ You need to be sure-footed and have a head for heights for this medium-difficulty hike.
Cable car daily 8am– 4.45/5.45/6.45pm (depending on season) 22 euros/pers | tel. 04 57 40 02 06 | funiviedelbaldo.it

Walking the old road to the village of Tremosine high above the western shore

A COFFEE AT THE SUMMIT

Even the trip up from the cable car station in Malcesine
➤ p. 54 is a feast for the eyes. The panoramic gondolas
rotate as they ascend, offering wonderful views of the
lake. Especially in summer, try to get to the lower
station as early as possible in order to avoid a long wait.
Once you're at the top, take in the fresh mountain air
and enjoy the amazing view from the terrace of the
❶ Monte Baldo cable car top station. Look to the
north to see the wild peaks of the Brenta Dolomites and
the snowy crests of Adamello and Presanella. Endless
mountain ridges stretch to the south, while the lake
laps onto the shore far below. You won't be the first to
sit down and order a cappuccino before taking off on
the day's adventure. Why wouldn't you enjoy enjoy a
relaxing start?

The approx. 30-km-long mountain ridge doesn't have a
summit as such, but rather several high peaks such as
Monte Altissimo di Nago (2,079m), Cima delle Pozzette
(2,132m), Cima Valdritta (2,218m) and Punta Telegrafo
(2,200m). Cima delle Pozzette is the first peak you
will reach after setting off from the cable car station.
Although the trail over the crest to this peak is not really

**❶ Monte Baldo
cable car top station**

200m   3mins

difficult, it is demanding enough to cause serious trouble for hikers wearing sandals.

From the cable car station, the trail climbs slightly and to the right, towards the south, past the cosy inn Baita dei Forti ➤ p. 58. *For the entire stretch, you should follow the red/white/red-marked path 651 that leads down into the trough of* ❷ Bocca di Tratto Spino (1,720 m).

❷ Bocca di Tratto Spino

The trail here is wide and easygoing, but the climb up the other side towards Punta Telegrafo follows a path that gets narrower between boulders. With a bit of luck, you might see a marmot or two in this area.

INSIDER TIP
Marmot Day

900m   25mins

FABULOUS ALPINE FLORA

The trail is rocky in parts but also crosses meadows and passes shrubs. Every now and then, you should stop and enjoy the view. Don't forget to take a closer look at the flora around you as well. This massif escaped the effects of the last Ice Age, which means that an overwhelming array of flowers and plants flourish here.

❸ Pra Alpesina chairlift top station

Especially in May and June, the peonies, tiger lilies and elderflowered orchids are in full bloom.

After walking for about half an hour, you will arrive at the ❸ *top station of the Pra Alpesina chairlift*, which connects Monte Baldo with Avio. Someone has sprayed painted in red the words "Bel Vedere" on the lift hut – the view is beautiful indeed! The trail continues fairly evenly over grass-covered ridges, across sprawling meadows and through pine groves. You can already see the rugged rocks of Cima delle Pozzette before you. The path alternates between stretches of meadow and rocky terrain.

After hiking for about an hour, you will come across a meadow to the right of

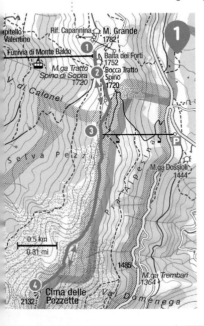

Cima delle Pozzette is a Monte Baldo highlight

the trail that is covered with countless cairns. This is the ideal spot to take a long break and build your own. To the left, you can see the Adige Valley and Rovereto below, and to the right Malcesine and the lake.

From here, the trail climbs steadily upwards. You now need to watch your step; the path leads through bushes and over large boulders, but is mostly dotted with rocks. You will gain height quickly before you come to a rugged ridge and then a saddle. *After about two or two and a half hours, you will reach your destination,* namely ❹ Cima delle Pozzette.

2350m 80mins

❹ Cima delle Pozzette

AN UNUSUAL SUMMIT CROSS

The cross on the summit is a curious feature: a rusty chair frame serves as the holder for a cross made of thick branches, held tight by a few stones and decorated with plastic flowers. The view of the lake about 2,000m below is breathtaking. By now, you have more than earned your sandwich. While tucking into your lunch, study the rocks of Val d'Angual and try to spot the chamois that can sometimes be seen darting over the rocks. *Follow the same trail back down to reach the* ❶ Monte Baldo cable car top station *in about an hour.*

3450m 80mins

❶ Monte Baldo cable car top station

❷ THROUGH THE SARCA VALLEY TO TRENTO & ROVERETO

➤ The barren Marocche: a moon-like landscape for climbers
➤ Admire giant dinosaur skeletons in the MuSe museum
➤ Discover the artworks of Italian futurists in Rovereto

📍 Torbole

🔁 Approx. 100km

🏁 Torbole

2 days
🚗 (2 hrs total driving time)

DAY 1
❶ Torbole

6km 5mins

❷ Arco

16km 1½hrs

❸ Marocche

9km 10mins

The route begins in ❶ Torbole ➤ p. 50. *After just a few miles,* you will come to the lively town of ❷ Arco ➤ p. 53, which is a worthwhile first stop. The pretty old town centre huddles close to a narrow cliff with the ruins of an ancient hilltop castle. In 1872, the Austrian emperor chose this town as the winter residence for his court because of the mild climate. Impressive villas, sweeping promenades and the botanical gardens are the remnants of this imperial past. Today, Arco is a popular destination among outdoor enthusiasts. Visit the Omkafè coffee museum, the Museo del Caffè *(Mon-Fri 8am-noon and 2.30-6.30pm, Sat 8am-noon | Via Aldo Moro 7 | omkafe.com)* and drink a cup of freshly brewed coffee.

THE BOULDERS OF THE MAROCCHE
Continue northwards through the Sarca Valley towards Dro. This region is particularly well known for its plums as well as *vino santo,* a white dessert wine produced from the Nosiola grape. After a few bends in the road, you will come to the wild-looking environs of ❸ Marocche. In primeval times, a massive landslide hit the valley, leaving enormous rocks scattered about as if giants had been playing with building blocks.

A BREAK AT THE CLIMBERS' MEETING PLACE
On the left-hand side at the foot of Monte Brento between Dro and Pietramurata, you will find the

Placche Zebrate. The so-called "sunny slabs" are up to 500m high and this is climbing territory. But some climbers also like to drink hot chocolate at ❹ Parete Zebrata *(closed Tue | Gaggiolo 4 | barparetezebrata.it)* and observe the activities on the rock face – or watch the free-falling base jumpers who dare to dive off Monte Brento.

❹ **Parete Zebrata**

7 km 5mins

LUNCH IN THE MOATED CASTLE

Afterwards, continue along the main road to ❺ Sarche. Visit the small but well-stocked supermarket at the crossroads to buy yourself a picnic lunch. You will find

❺ **Sarche**

tasty delicacies ranging from pickled asparagus, cheese and salami to raspberry jam and bakery goods. If you ask nicely, one of the employees will make you a panino to order. The next stop, just a stone's throw away, is ⑥ Lago di Toblino. Sitting on an island, *which you can reach by walking across a dam,* you will find a moated castle with distinctive towers. Originally from the 12th century, the castle was transformed into a comfortable residential palace in the 16th century. Today, it houses a good restaurant: Ristorante Castel Toblino *(closed Mon/Tue and Nov–Feb | Via Caffaro 1 | tel. 04 61 86 40 36 | casteltoblino.com | €€–€€€).*

2km 5mins

⑥ **Lago di Toblino**

17km 20mins

⑦ **Trento**

A CAPPUCCINO IN ONE OF ITALY'S MOST BEAUTIFUL SQUARES

About 20km further on, you will come to ⑦ Trento (pop. 115,000). For centuries, this beautiful city situated between the Dolomite mountains and Lake Garda has been a melting pot of Italian, German and Austrian culture. It combines the Italian "Dolce Vita" with a dose of central European pragmatism. Let yourself be carried away along the streets of the romantic Old Town and enjoy the palaces, churches and shop windows that await. One of the city's landmarks is the Baroque Neptune fountain from 1768 on the cathedral square, one of the most beautiful *piazzas* in Italy. For the best view over the heart of the city, head to Caffè Italia *(Piazza Duomo 7).*

Trento's magnificent cathedral square is a great place to enjoy a drink

Once you have regained your strength, *take a ten-minute walk* to the ★ 👥 Museo delle Scienze MuSe *(Tue–Fri 10am–6pm, Sat/Sun 10am–7pm | Corso del Lavoro e della Scienza 3 | muse.it).* In Italy's most modern museum of natural sciences, visitors of all ages can explore the earth from the African bush to the glaciers of the Alps with the help of virtual exhibits. You can also inspect the huge dinosaur skeletons. If you are interested in visiting all three museums in Trento and Rovereto, which are described on this tour, it is worth getting a  *museum pass (22 euros | short.travel/gar27).* Use it to avoid queuing at the entrance to numerous museums and castles in the entire Trentino. In addition, it includes free public transport in Trento and Rovereto for 48 hours.

DINNER IN A CENTURIES-OLD OSTERIA

For a centrally located, yet inexpensive place to stay, check out Hotel Venezia *(hotelveneziatn.it).* Ask for a room with a view of the cathedral! In the evening, head to Ristorante al Vò *(closed Sun | Vicolo del Vò 11 | tel. 04 61 98 5374 | ristorantealvo.it | €€).* An older restaurant would be hard to find – this, Trento's first *osteria,* opened its doors in 1345; today, the it serves traditional Trentino cuisine.

The next day, take the SS12 to ❽ Rovereto (pop. 38,000). Not only the Venetian castle that sits above the lively streets of the Old Town, but also the mix of Italian Palazzi and Austrian architecture attest to the once strategic position of the Rovereto. Until 1919, this town in the Adige Valley belonged to the Austrian Empire and it was bitterly contested during World War I. For more details about the town's history during the war, head to the Museo Storico Italiano della Guerra *(Tue–Sun 10am–6pm; July/Sept Sat/Sun until 7pm | Via Castelbarco 7 | museodellaguerra.it).*

EXCITING ART IN A SPECTACULAR BUILDING

It is the fusion of the past, present and future that makes Rovereto so interesting. You can experience this yourself by visiting the ultra-modern ★ Museo di Arte Moderna e Contemporanea di Trento e Rovereto MART *(Tue–Sun 10am–6pm (Fri until 9pm) | Corso Bettini 43 | mart.tn.it).* The main focus of this modern art museum is Italian art from the 20th and 21st centuries. The museum also holds one of the most important collections of futuristic art in Italy. The building itself

29km 1½hrs

DAY 2

❽ **Rovereto**

16km 20mins

was designed by the Ticino architect Mario Botta, who was faced with the daunting task of constructing a large modern building in the midst of a densely built historic city centre. He arranged the three storeys of the museum around a huge, circular agora topped with a glass dome. This central space can accommodate events for up to 1,200 visitors.

From Rovereto, it only takes *about 30 minutes on the SS240,* to get back to the lake. *Before the road winds up to the Passo San Giovanni (287m),* it is well worth stopping at the ❾ Lago di Loppio. This protected wetlands area, which only resembles a lake after heavy rainfall, is extremely peaceful and the perfect place to stretch your legs one last time before returning to ❶ Torbole ➤ p. 50.

❾ **Lago di Loppio**

7km   10mins

❶ **Torbole**

The circular agora in Mario Botta's ultra-modern MART museum

❸ TO THE HEIGHTS OF TREMOSINE & TIGNALE

➤ The Strada della Forra: Lake Garda's most spectacular road
➤ Delicious Alpine cheese at the Alpe del Garda
➤ From the lake's shore, go high up into the mountains

📍 Limone

🔄 Approx. 55 km

🏁 Limone

🚗 1 day (60–90 mins total driving time)

❶ Limone

8km 10mins

❷ Strada della Forra

2km 5mins

❸ La Forra

1km 5mins

❹ Pieve

Start off from ❶ Limone sul Garda ➤ p. 42 and *turn right off the Gardesana Occidentale before you reach Campione, to head towards Tremosine*. The curvy panoramic SP38 road, known as ❷ ★ Strada della Forra, leads through the narrow Brasa canyon up to Pieve. Winston Churchill enthusiastically called this road the "eighth wonder of the world", and Daniel Craig, alias James Bond, filmed a scene from *Quantum of Solace* in front of this impressive backdrop. If you look up from the lake to the houses of Pieve, which stand on a high plateau around 350m above the water, you can't help but wonder how a road could wind up to this town. It is a true masterpiece of engineering and a one-of-a-kind panoramic experience. This road is very narrow indeed, so it is advisable to be patient and drive carefully.

A PASTA OR PIZZA BREAK

After about 2km, take your first break. *Just after the canyon narrows considerably, park your car on the left* at the restaurant ❸ La Forra *(closed Thu | Via Benaco 24 | tel. 03 65 91 81 66 | laforra.com | €)* and explore the area on foot. If your stomach is rumbling, make a pit stop at the restaurant. The pizza comes straight from the wood-fired oven and the home-made pasta is delicious.

A 300-M-HIGH PLATFORM ABOVE THE LAKE

Wait though until you get to nearby ❹ Pieve ➤ p. 116 to enjoy a cup of coffee on one of the two "swaying

terraces". The Hotel Paradiso sits directly on the edge above the lake and the large terrace sits on a platform that juts out from the cliff, offering a view of the lake about 300m below. If the weather isn't great, the nearby Ristorante Miralago has a kind of free-floating, panoramic winter garden. Afterwards, take a stroll through the historic centre of Pieve in which many of the 18th-century houses have been lovingly restored.

If you are a fan of truffles, ask at the tourist information office for Luca – he sometimes has a few of these prized delicacies for sale in the autumn. Continue through the wild hillsides and pine forests, across green plateaux and past olive groves to the dairy ❺ Alpe del Garda ➤ p. 116 in Polzone. All the crossroads have signs pointing the way to the dairy. In summer it offers free guided tours and cheese-tasting (Thu–Tue 11am and 4pm). There is also a restaurant and a nicely stocked shop with milk products from the dairy – the raw milk cheese is really good – as well as other local delicacies such as salami, honey and olive oil. It's a good place to stock up on picnic provisions.

INSIDER TIP
Fresh cheese for sale

8km 30mins	
❺ Alpe del Garda	
10km 10mins	

A SMALL CHURCH ON A STEEP ROCK

The panoramic road continues towards Tignale. Far from the hustle and bustle around Lake Garda, this road leads through untouched mountainous countryside. *Before you reach Gardola, turn left* to get to the pilgrimage church of ❻ Madonna di Montecastello ➤ p. 115, which was built in the 17th century. Like an eagle's nest, it clings to the top of a steep cliff that drops almost 700m straight down. After visiting the church, it is worth

❻ Madonna di Montecastello	
1km 20mins	

hiking about 20 minutes up to the peak of ❼ **Monte Castello**: *Turn left and go past the church, following the signs "alla croce", to the cross at the top.* Enjoy the unparalleled views of the lake along the path.

If you would like to learn more about the Alto Garda Nature Park, you should make one last stop at the small ❽ **Museo del Parco Alto Garda Bresciano** *(Sun–Mon, Wed–Fri 2–6pm, Sat 1–6pm | parcoaltogarda.it)* in Prabione. It explains how the mountains on the edge of Lake Garda were formed and tells of the lives of the local residents. The nature park is full of contrasts, especially because it stretches from a height of 65m on the lakeshore up to a height of almost 2,000m. It is really not surprising that the climate and vegetation, as well as social and economic conditions, vary greatly within the park. *Go through Oldesio and Piovere to head back down to the lake and along Gardesana Occidentale to* ❶ Limone.

❼ Monte Castello

3km · 20mins

❽ Museo del Parco Alto Garda Bresciano

24km · 25mins

❶ Limone

❹ CYCLING ALONG THE BANKS OF THE RIVER MINCIO

➤ Enjoy Lake Garda's best brioches for breakfast
➤ Cycle past floodplain forest and storks
➤ Feast on tortellini in their 'native habitat'

📍 Peschiera   🏁 Peschiera

🔄 33km   🚴 1 day (2½ hrs total cycling time)

📶 easy   ↗ 50m

ℹ Bike hire: *Noleggio Bici Piccoli Mauro (13 euros/day, children 6.50 euros | Via Venezia 15 | tel. 34 94 67 80 06 | noleggiobicilettepeschieradelgarda.it)*

❶ Peschiera

9km 40mins

This tour begins in true Italian style in ❶ Peschiera del Garda ➤ p.79, with a cappuccino and a freshly made brioche (sweet or savoury) at Torta della Nonna *(closed Thu | Via Risorgimento 5). Go through the old town centre towards the fortress to get to the river, which is where the bike trail starts.* The Mincio is in fact the only river that drains from Lake Garda, and it flows into the River Po 50km to the south, near Governolo. Since the river was a natural line of defence in centuries past, it was of great strategic importance. As you cycle through the quiet countryside with its meadows and vineyards, it is hard to believe that bitter battles took place here during the Italian War of Independence against Austria in the 19th century. However, castles, city walls and watchtowers along the riverbanks are testimony to this history.

BIRDS, ANGLERS & FLOODPLAIN FOREST
The well-marked bike path meanders under shady trees through the countryside marked by floodplain forests. Countless bird species and over 300 kinds of plants

The River Mincio still powers mill wheels in idyllic Borghetto

flourish along the banks of the river and the white stork has been successfully reintroduced. Many anglers treasure the untouched nature on these shores.

After about an hour, the mighty church of the seemingly sleepy village of ❷ Monzambano rises before you. It is time for a stop, so *cross over the bridge to follow the path up to the village centre.* Grab a bite to eat at Caffè Frapporti *(closed Mon | Piazza Vittorio Emanuele).* Enjoy the impressive view from the watchtowers of the Castello over the peaceful riverside to Lake Garda. *Afterwards, hop back on the saddle and return to the bike path.*

WOODEN WHEELS
OF OLD WATERMILLS

Soon you will see the mighty walls and towers of the 600-m-long, fortress-like dam wall, Ponte Visconteo ➤ p. 81, and the towers of the impressive castle of Valeggio. First, visit the old part of ❸ Borghetto ➤ p. 81 with its medieval mill district. Time seems to have stood still here, and you can still see the wooden wheels of the old watermills.

If you are hungry now, cycle on to the neighbouring ❹ Valeggio sul Mincio and taste the handmade pasta dishes in Trattoria Il Cavallino *(closed Thu | Via Giuseppe Verdi 8 | tel. 04 57 95 11 38 | €€),* away from the tourist throng. For a dolce, though, you should treat yourself to something sweet at Pastificio Remelli. *Then it is time to retrace the same path back to* ❶ Peschiera.

❷ Monzambano	
7km	30mins
❸ Borghetto	
1km	5mins
❹ Valeggio sul Mincio	
15km	1hr
❶ Peschiera	

GOOD TO KNOW

HOLIDAY BASICS

ARRIVAL

GETTING THERE
AIR

Verona's Valerio Catullo *(aeroporto verona.it)* is the closest *airport* to Lake Garda. A number of airlines offer regular flights from cities around the UK. You can also fly to Venice, Milan or Bergamo.

No trains run from Verona airport into the city, but the *aerobus* runs every 20 minutes from the terminal to Verona's main train station, Porta Nuova. A single ticket costs 6 euros. Trains run from the main station to Trento, Rovereto and Lake Garda. From mid-July to mid-September, bus 164 runs hourly along the eastern short of the lake via Peschiera to Garda (connections to Riva); a single ticket costs 3.50–6 euros, depending on your destination *(atv.verona.it)*.

There are also private shuttle services, e.g. Europlan *(europlan.it/ transfer)* or Lake Garda Transfer *(lake- gardatransfers.it)*, and many hotels and campsites offer their own airport shuttle service.

CAR

To reach Lake Garda from the UK by car, you will most likely travel to Calais and through France and Switzerland and then take the A4 Milan–Venice motorway (exit: Desenzano, Sirmione and Peschiera). You will need a vignette if you use the Swiss motorways, and tolls are charged on motorways in France and Italy.

TRAIN & COACH

The quickest way from the UK by train is with the Eurostar via Paris and then on to Milan. Intercity and Eurocity trains link other European cities with main Italian destinations. Italy's dense

Sentiero Ponale from Riva into the Ledro Valley: a spectacular mountain-bike trail

rail network, reasonable ticket prices and reliable train schedules make travelling by rail an excellent way of getting around. For further information, go to: *raileurope.com, italiarail.com, eurostar.com, rome2rio.com* and *seat61.com*

You can also travel from the UK to Lake Garda by coach, e.g. London to Pescheria, in approx. 28 hours.

GETTING IN

If you are travelling from the UK, you will need a passport that was issued less than 10 years before the date you enter Italy (check the "date of issue"). It must also be valid for at least three months after the date you intend to leave Italy (check the "expiry date"). Citizens of the US or Canada currently require a visa only if staying for longer than three months.

CLIMATE & WHEN TO GO

winter, the temperature seldom dips below freezing point. Only a few hotels are open, but this is when the west shore displays its fin-de-siècle charm. When there is snow in the mountains and it's foggy on the damp Po plain, you may still be able to go for a walk in the sun by Lake Garda. Spring is perhaps the best time to visit the lake: the mild climate is perfect for hiking, the hotel prices are still moderate (except at Easter) and you can easily find somewhere to stay. However, the water is still chilly – bathing is generally best between mid-May and late September. In summer it can get hot although the wind off the lake makes the temperature more bearable. The one drawback is that everyone in northern Italy seems to spend their holidays here. Weekends in August are bumper-to-bumper time: mile-long traffic jams with stop-and-go on the roads and body contact on the beaches. Autumn is perfect for hiking. Weeks of stable weather are not unusual and from the top of Monte Baldo you can see to Verona and beyond.

GETTING AROUND

BUS

It cannot be repeated enough: leave your car in the hotel car park and use public transport! The roads around the lake are chronically jammed. The bus trip from Riva to Limone costs less than 2 euros – parking in Limone costs 1 euro an hour. Bus timetables can be obtained from all tourist offices and the buses are fairly punctual – traffic permitting. Tickets *(biglietti)* have to be bought before the start of the journey; in the larger villages from the ticket office at the bus station or else from tobacconists. You can also buy tickets on the bus – but you will have to pay almost double. *ttspa.it* (Trentino), *atv.verona.it* (Veneto, *bresciamobilita.it* (Lombardy)

CAR HIRE

There are car rental firms *(autonoleggio)* – both the big international and local companies – in many towns around the lake. It is recommended that you book in advance for the high season. Generally, this is also the cheaper alternative, for example via Internet brokers.

DRIVING

The maximum speed in built-up areas is 50kmh, on main roads 90kmh, on dual carriageways 110kmh, and 130kmh on motorways. It is mandatory to drive with dipped headlights during the day (outside built-up areas); this applies to motorbike and moped riders everywhere. The blood alcohol limit is 0.5. There must be an emergency jacket for each passenger in the car which has to be worn if you leave the car due to a breakdown or an accident outside built-up areas. In Italy there are very strict rules to be observed and traffic offenders will feel the full weight of the law: alcohol is absolutely prohibited under the age of 21 and during the first three years of someone possessing a driving licence. Those who have just passed their test are not allowed to drive faster than 90kmh on main roads or 100kmh on motorways. Anyone cycling after dark outside of built-up areas must wear a high-visibility jacket or warning stripes. Charges are almost always levied when parking in a town and the police hand out tickets with great enthusiasm. With the exception of those located on motorways, most petrol stations close for lunch and on Sundays, although many do have credit card-operated pumps. Breakdown service (toll-free number): *tel. 80 31 16*, from non-Italian mobile phones *8 00 11 68 00*.

FERRY ⚑

Ferries are a nice, albeit slightly slower, alternative for circumnavigating the lake. The car ferries Maderno–Torri del

FESTIVALS & EVENTS
ALL YEAR ROUND

EASTER
Good Friday procession (Limone)

MAY
1,000-mile rally Mille Miglia (photo), *1000miglia.it*
Bike Festival (Riva), *riva.bike-festival.de/en*

JUNE
Festa del Nodo d'Amore (Valeggio sul Mincio): Open-air tortellini festival, *ristorantivaleggio.it*

JUNE-SEPTEMBER
Opera festival (Verona), *arena.it*

JULY
Drodesera Fies Festival (Dro): Theatre festival in an old hydropower station, *centralefies.it*
Sardellata al Chiar di Luna (Garda): Festival of the Lake Garda sardine

JULY/AUGUST
Garda Jazz Festival (Riva), *gardajazz.com*

AUGUST
Aperitivo sotto le stelle (Bardolino): The shoreline promenade is turned into an open-air bar, *degustibus.org*
Notte di Fiaba (Riva): Theater, music and games with a big fireworks display, *nottedifiaba.it*

SEPTEMBER
Dance festival Oriente Occidente (Rovereto), *orienteoccidente.it*
Sailing Regatta Centomiglia (Gargnano), *centomiglia.it*
Ciottolando con Gusto (Malcesine): Wine tastings and culinary stalls, *ciottolando.com*

OCTOBER
Lake Garda Marathon, *lakegardamarathon.com*
Festa dell'Uva e del Vino (Bardolino): Wine festival, *bardolinotop.it*

DECEMBER
New Year's Eve party HOP! (Riva), *hoprivadelgarda.com*

Cheap and cheerful: a glass of red wine and a serving of gnocchi

Benaco (every hour during the day) and Limone–Malcesine (10 times a day during peak season) save you driving halfway round the lake. During the peak season a car ferry operates between Riva and Desenzano, only stopping at a few places. Passenger ferries between Desenzano and Riva stop at many places en route. In the summer season, there are evening cruises. Timetables are available from the tourist information offices and where the boats come in; you can also buy advance tickets here. *navlaghi.it*

EMERGENCIES

CONSULATES & EMBASSIES
BRITISH CONSULATE GENERAL
Via S. Paolo 7 | Milan | tel. 02 72 30 01 | gov.uk/government/world/organisa tions/british-embassy-rome/office/ british-consulate-general-milan

U.S. CONSULATE GENERAL
Via Principe Amedeo 2/10 | Milan | tel. 02 29 03 51 | it.usembassy.gov/ embassyconsulates/milan

CONSULATE OF CANADA
Piazza Cavour 3 Milano | canada international.gc.ca/italy-italie

EMERGENCY SERVICES
Call *112* for the police, ambulance, fire brigade and mountain rescue.

HEALTH
Before you travel, it is advisable to take out international health insurance; that way you can choose your doctor, pay in cash, get a receipt and then present your bills to your insurance company for a refund. During the summer season the emergency doctor, the *Guardia Medica Turistica*, is on stand-by to look after holidaymakers.

ESSENTIALS

BEACHES

Lake Garda beaches are usually pebbly. Water quality and bathing safety are monitored during the official season from May to September. Dogs are not always welcome; and not all beaches are clothing-optional. On the eastern and western shores, in particular, the beaches are often narrow or located below the main road.

CAMPING

Some shores around Lake Garda are more suitable for camping than others; there is too little space in the north due to the sheer rock faces. Most camp sites are in the south, especially in Valtenesi between Desenzano and Salò, and most are of a good standard. The price per night is usually around 18 euros for the site, 10 euros per adult and 8 euros per child.

CUSTOMS

Travellers from other EU countries are subject to very few customs rules. However, if travelling from the UK and other non-EU countries you will need to check your allowances before bringing things in or out of the country. When flying into Italy, non-EU citizens require an onward or return ticket.

DISCOUNT CARDS & PASSES

You can save money with the 🐟 *Garda Promotions Card*. You get discounts in musuems and leisure parks, such as Vittoriale, Parco Natura Viva, the Arena in Verona, Gardaland and Canevaworld. Reductions are also given for boat trips and the cable car from Malcesine to Monte Baldo. The card is available for free in tourist offices and most hotels.

If you are travelling in the Trentino and want to visit several museums, the *museum pass (22 euros | short. travel/gar27)* is worthwhile. It allows you to use all public transport in Trento and Rovereto and to visit three dozen museums and castles in the region over a period of 48 hours.

HOW MUCH DOES IT COST?	
Coffee	*1.50–3 euros for a cappuccino*
Snack	*from 3.50 euros for a filled panino*
Wine	*1–1.80 euros for a glass at a bar*
Olive oil	*from 15 euros for 1 litre olio extravergine*
Petrol	*around 1.60 euros for 1 litre Super Euro 95*
Cable car	*22 euros for a return trip up and down Monte Baldo*

ENTRY FEES & PRICES

At tourist attractions like the MART in Rovereto, the Giardino Botanico André Heller or Vittoriale in Gardone expect to pay 11–16 euros. For the Grotte di Catullo or the castle in Sirmione as well as for Cascata del Varone in Riva, entry costs 5–6 euros. Amusement parks like Gardaland are expensive (from 37 euros). Many museums offer free entry for under 12s and over 60s.

INFORMATION
VISITGARDA TOURIST INFORMATION
Trentino: *Largo Medaglie d'Oro 5 | 38066 Riva del Garda | tel. 04 64 55 44 44 | gardatrentino.it*
Veneto: *Lungolago Regina Adelaide 3 | 37016 Garda | tel. 04 57 25 52 79 | lagodigardaveneto.com*
Lombardy: *Via Oliva 32 | 25084 Gargnano | tel. 03 65 79 11 72 | gardalombardia.com*

ITALIAN GOVERNMENT TOURIST BOARD (ENIT)
In the UK: *1 Princes Street, W1B 2AY London, tel. 020 7408 1254*
In the US: *686 Park Ave, 3rd Floor, New York, NY 10065, tel. 212-245 5618*
In Canada: *365 Bay Street, Suite 503, Toronto M5H 2V1, tel. 416-925 48 82*

MONEY & CREDIT CARDS
Cash machines *(bancomat)* are available everywhere and the usual credit cards are accepted at petrol stations, virtually all hotels, most restaurants and in many shops.

OPENING HOURS
Opening hours are not uniformly regulated in Italy but shops are usually open Monday–Saturday 9am–noon and 3.30–7pm; larger supermarkets usually have no lunch break. In many towns the shops in the pedestrian precincts are open until 10pm or later.

Most grocery stores are also open on Sunday morning.

POST
Stamps *(francobolli)* are available from post offices and tobacconists *(tabacchi)* but hardly ever where you buy the postcards!

PUBLIC HOLIDAYS

1 Jan	Capodanno (New Year)
6 Jan	Epifania (Epiphany)
March/April	Pasqua and Pasquetta (Easter Sunday and Easter Monday)
25 April	Liberazione (Anniversary of the Liberation from Fascism)
1 May	Festa del Lavoro (Labour Day)
2 June	Festa della Repubblica (national holiday)
15 Aug	Ferragosto (Mid-August)
1 Nov	Ognissanti (All Saints' Day)
8 Dec	Immacolata Concezione (Immaculate Conception)
25 Dec	Natale (Christmas)
26 Dec	Santo Stefano (St Stephen's feast day)

TELEPHONE & WIFI
The country code for Italy is +39. You have to dial the 0 at the beginning of each landline connection – both from abroad and when making local calls. Mobile telephone numbers (often 338 or 339) are always dialled without a 0. Country codes from Italy are +44 (UK), +1 (US and Canada) and +353 (Ireland). Telephone cards can be purchased in most *tabacchi* shops. Most British mobile phones work without a problem in Italy.

Most hotels and some restaurants in Italy will provide free WiFi although it may be slow. Many municipalities have set up WiFi hotspots for those who have an Italian SIM card (all others have to register with a credit card and pay 3 euros per day or 10 euros per week). *Free Luna (freeluna.it)* is a free network covering the northern Lake Garda region; Bardolino provides free access through the *Comune di Bardolino* network.

TIPPING

A fixed service charge is normally included in the bill. This charge generally replaces the less usual tip in Italy. On Lake Garda, however, the northern tradition for tipping and the Italian custom of charging a *coperto* have been combined, so that a tip is more usual but by no means expected. First,

RESPONSIBLE TRAVEL

Are you aware of your carbon footprint while travelling? You can offset your emissions (myclimate. org), plan your route with the environment in mind (routerank.com) and go gently on both nature and culture. As a tourist it is especially important to respect nature, look out for local products, cycle instead of driving, save water and much more. To find out more, please visit: ecotourism.org

always ensure you receive your change. Then you can leave the tip on the little tray with the bill.

WEATHER IN RIVA

High season
Low season

	JAN	FEB	MARCH	APRIL	MAY	JUNE	JULY	AUG	SEPT	OCT	NOV	DEC
Daytime temperature	5°	7°	12°	17°	20°	24°	27°	26°	22°	16°	11°	6°
Night-time temperature	1°	1°	4°	9°	13°	17°	19°	18°	15°	10°	5°	2°
☀ Hours of sunshine per day	3	4	5	5	6	7	8	7	6	6	3	3
🌂 Rainy days per month	5	5	7	9	11	10	8	8	7	8	8	6
≋ Lake temperature in °C	8	6	8	10	13	18	20	21	19	16	12	10

☀ Hours of sunshine per day   🌂 Rainy days per month   ≋ Lake temperature in °C

WORDS & PHRASES
IN ITALIAN

SMALLTALK

We have indicated the stressed vowel by a dot under the vowel.

yes/no/maybe	sì/no/forse
please/thank you	per favore/grazie
Excuse me/sorry!	Scusa!/Scusi!
Pardon?	Come dice?/Prego?
Good morning/good day/good evening/good night!	Buon giorno!/Buon giorno!/Buona sera!/Buona notte!
Hello/Bye/Goodbye!	Ciao!/Ciao!/Arrivederci!
My name is …	Mi chiamo …
What is your name? (formal/informal)	Come si chiama?/Come ti chiami?
I would like … /Do you have …?	Vorrei …/Avete …?
I (don't) like this	(Non) mi piace.
good/bad	buono/cattivo

SYMBOLS

EATING & DRINKING

The menu, please!	Il menù, per favore.
bottle/jug/glass	bottiglia/caraffa/bicchiere
knife/fork/spoon	coltello/forchetta/cucchiaio
salt/pepper/sugar	sale/pepe/zucchero
vinegar/oil/milk/cream/lemon	aceto/olio/latte/panna/limone
with/without ice/fizz (in water)	con/senza ghiaccio/gas
cold/too salty/undercooked	freddo/troppo salato/non cotto
vegetarian/allergy	vegetariano/vegetariana/allergia
I would like to pay, please	Vorrei pagare, per favore.
bill/receipt/tip	conto/ricevuta/mancia
cash/debit card/credit card	in contanti/carta di debito/carta di credito

MISCELLANEOUS

Where can I find ... ?	Dove posso trovare ...?
left/right/straight	sinistra/destra/dritto
What time is it?	Che ora è? Che ore sono?
it's three o'clock/ it's half three	Sono le tre./Sono le tre e mezza.
today/tomorrow/yesterday	oggi/domani/ieri
How much is ...?	Quanto costa ...?
too much/much/little/everything/ nothing	troppo/molto/poco/tutto/niente
expensive/cheap/price	caro/economico/prezzo
Where can I get internet/WiFi?	Dove trovo un accesso internet/ wi-fi?
open/closed	aperto/chiuso
broken/it's not working	guasto/non funziona
broken down/garage	guasto/officina
schedule/tickets	orario/biglietto
train/tracks/platform	treno/binario/banchina
Help!/Look out!/Be careful!	Aiuto!/Attenzione!/Prudenza!
ban/forbidden/danger/dangerous	divieto/vietato/pericolo/ pericoloso
pharmacy/drug store	farmacia
fever/pain	febbre/dolori
0/1/2/3/4/5/6/7/8/9/10/ 100/1000	zero/uno/due/tre/quattro/cinque / sei/sette/otto/nove/dieci/cento/ mille

HOLIDAY VIBES
FOR RELAXATION & CHILLING

FOR BOOKWORMS & FILM BUFFS

🎥 CALL ME BY YOUR NAME
The 2017, Oscar-nominated film by Luca Guadagnino shows scenes of Sirmione with its Jamaica Beach and Roman villa. Admittedly, these scenes only last for a couple of minutes, but Lake Garda residents are still proud of their region's appearance!

📖 TWILIGHT IN ITALY
In 1912, the English writer DH Lawrence hiked across the Alps to Italy and stayed in Gargnano with his lover. In this work he describes the days he spent on Lake Garda.

🎥 QUANTUM OF SOLACE
The 22nd Bond film, directed by Marc Forster (2010), starts with 007 (Daniel Craig) steering his Aston Martin in a wild car chase along the Gardesana road and through the Torbole and Tremosine tunnels.

PLAYLIST

0:58

II ARES ADAMI – STEPPING HIGHER
Gripping rap lines straight from Arco – great for dancing!

▶ LUCIANO BERETTA – LAGO DI GARDA GIOIELLO D'ITALY
This song has been the hymn of the community of Garda since 2013

▶ VAGABONDA – AL CARNEVAL
Folk from Costermano with guitar, violin, bass and accordion

▶ FAY HALLAM – ARCO
The queen of the English Mod scene sings about her love for Arco

▶ MEN OF LAKE – I DON'T WANT TO KNOW
A progressive rock band from Riva which composed some great songs in the 1980s and 1990s

▶ THE BASTARD SONS OF DIONISO – AMOR CARNALE
Trentino Italian rock band who climbed to no 1 in the charts in 2009

Your holiday soundtrack can be found on **Spotify** under **MARCO POLO** Italy

Or scan this code with the Spotify app

ON LINE

@INSTAGARDA
Not yet in the holiday mood? This Instagram page provides inspiration for your trip to Lake Garda, with especially picturesque town views.

PARCO FLUVIALE DELLA SARCA
This app shows cycle paths and hiking trails *(percorsi tematici)*, bus stops with cycle transport *(muoviti sostenibile)* and farms *(produttori Km0)* along the River Sarca. It's in Italian, but with the map it's easy to navigate.

BENNIE THE LAKE GARDA MONSTER
Lake Garda = Loch Ness?! For several years now, a group of people have attempted to prove that a monster called Bennie lives in Lake Garda. benniefanclub.com tells you all you want to know about this friendly dinosaur.

SHORT.TRAVEL/GAR15
A guided canyoning tour through the Rio Nero Canyon in Ledro Valley which will inspire you to set off immediately!

TRAVEL PURSUIT
THE MARCO POLO HOLIDAY QUIZ

Do you know your facts about Lake Garda? Here you can test your knowledge of the little secrets and idiosyncrasies of the region and its people. You will find the correct answers below, with further details on pages 18 to 23 of this guide.

❶ How many tunnels are on the Gardesana Occidentale between Riva and Gargnano?
a) 34
b) 52
c) 74

❷ Which local speciality became a motif on stamps?
a) Lake Garda trout *(carpione)*
b) Dried cod *(bacclà alla vicentina)*
c) Lake Garda olive oil

❸ Which treasures can be unearthed at Monte Baldo?
a) Manganese
b) Gold
c) Truffles

❹ In which village on the lake do the residents live to a particularly ripe old age?
a) Limone
b) Malcesine
c) Garda

❺ What do you call the coldest days in the year on Lake Garda?
a) Blackbird days *(giorni della merla)*
b) Magpie days *(giorni della gazza)*
c) Pigeon days *(giorni del piccione)*

❻ What is the special ingredient in the crumbly *torta sbrisolona*?
a) Cinnamon
b) Saffron
c) Raisins marinated in Bardolino

Answers: 1c, 2b, 3c, 4a, 5a, 6b, 7b, 8c, 9c, 10a, 11b, 12c

Magical lemons: the yellow fruits grow in and around Limone

❼ When was the Gardesana Occidentale built?
a) At the end of the 19th century
b) After World War I
c) In the 1960s

❽ How many kilograms of olives do two experienced pickers collect in a day?
a) 50kg
b) 75kg
c) 100kg

❾ How does fisherman Alberto Rania notify his customers of his daily offering?
a) He stands in Riva market square speaking through a megaphone
b) Via circular email
c) Via WhatsApp

❿ What lies on the lakebed between Maderno and Torri del Benaco?
a) A 17th-century cargo vessel
b) Some 2nd-century Roman coins
c) A 28-ton boulder from the last Ice Age

⓫ What is covered in plastic sheeting in some lakeside towns in winter?
a) Young olive trees before they shoot
b) Parking meters
c) Lemon trees in the *limonaie*

⓬ To what do the Italians liken the residents of Trento?
a) Moody ibex
b) Stubborn donkeys
c) Grumpy bears

INDEX

WE WANT TO HEAR FROM YOU!

Did you have a great holiday? Is there something on your mind? Whatever it is, let us know! Whether you want to praise the guide, alert us to errors or give us a personal tip – MARCO POLO would be pleased to hear from you.
Please contact us by email:

sales@heartwoodpublishing.co.uk

We do everything we can to provide the very latest information for your trip. Nevertheless, despite all of our authors' thorough research, errors can creep in. MARCO POLO does not accept any liability for this.

PICTURE CREDITS
Cover photo: Limone sul Garda (Schapowalow: D. Erbetta)
Photos: Fotos: M. Bettoni (147); Getty Images: F. Vallenari (20/21); Getty Images/Kontributor: F. Bienewald (55); huber-images: M. Arduino (77), C. Bäck (142/143), U. Bernhart (23), F. Cogoli (88), O. Fantuz (80), Gräfenhain (2/3, 42), G. Gräfenhain (45), Huber (112), H. P. Huber (12/13, 19, 114), H. Klaes (78), K. Kreder (51), F. Lukasseck (24/25), S. Raccanello (27, 28, 65), TC (49), S. Termanini (102); Laif: F. Blickle (111), Celentano (35), M. Galli (30/31, 97, 144/145), T. Gerber (11, 93), Gollhardt/Wieland (115/116), G. Heidorn (53), B. Steinhilber (81, 126), C. Zahn (103), H. D. Zinn (60/61); Laif/Le Figaro Magazine: Sander (31); E. Sander (6/7); Laif/SZ Photo: J. Giribas (56/57); Look: I. Pompe (9, 58), A. Strauß (outside cover flap), H. Wohner (68/69), K. Wothe (90/91); mauritius imager/Imagebroker (32/33), A. Reinert (98/99); Siepmann (121); mauritius images: U. Bernhart (84/85, 106/107), R. Kaessmann (38/39), mauritius images/Alamy (130, 135), J. Bracegirdle (95, 108), H. Corneli (67, 71), MARKA (72, 109), R. Proctor (124), S. Vidler (inside cover flap), mauritius images/CuboImages (10); mauritius images/foodcollection (26/27); mauritius images/SFM ITALY E/Alamy (74/75); mauritius images/Shopping/Alamy: P. Forsberg (8); mauritius images/Travel Collection: T. Langlotz (83, 118/119, 132/133); T. Stankiewicz (14/15); vario images/Westend61 (136)

11th Edition – fully revised and updated 2023
Worldwide Distribution: Heartwood Publishing Ltd, Bath, United Kingdom
www.heartwoodpublishing.co.uk

Authors: Margherita Bettoni, Barbara Schaefer
Editor: Nikolai Michaelis
Picture editor: Stefanie Wiese

Cartography: © MAIRDUMONT, Ostfildern (pp. 36–37, 123, 128, 131, pull-out map; Kompass Karten GmbH, A-Innsbruck © MAIRDUMONT, Ostfildern (p. 120); © MAIRDUMONT, Ostfildern, using data from OpenStreetMap, licence CC-BY-SA 2.0 (pp. 40–41, 42, 62–63, 73, 86–87, 89, 94, 100–101, 104)

Cover design and pull-out map cover design: bilekjaeger_Kreativagentur with Zukunftswerkstatt, Stuttgart
Page design: Langenstein Communication GmbH, Ludwigsburg

Heartwood Publishing credits:
Translated from the German by Thomas Moser, Christopher Wynne, Jennifer Walcoff Neuheiser and Suzanne Kirkbright,
Editors: Felicity Laughton, Kate Michell, Sophie Blacksell Jones
Prepress: Summerlane Books, Bath
Printed in India

MARCO POLO AUTHOR
MARGHERITA BETTONI
Originally from Lake Garda, Margherita Bettoni never really thought of herself as being particularly proud of her homeland. That is, until the day when colleagues at the German School for Journalists in Munich pointed out that she enthused about the *lago* and its surroundings at least once a day. Today, the freelance journalist lives in northern Germany but visits Lake Garda as often as she can.

DOS & DON'TS

HOW TO AVOID SLIP-UPS & BLUNDERS

DON'T ARRIVE DURING FERRAGOSTO
If at all possible, do not travel to Lake Garda around 15 August! That is when all of Italy is on holiday and the traffic comes to a standstill. It is usually just as packed on the beaches around the lake.

DON'T ORDER IN ENGLISH EVERYWHERE YOU GO
Of course, most Lake Garda waiters will understand you when you order "a beer". But how about learning a handful of Italian words? Drawing the waiter's attention with a polite *scusi* – excuse me – is almost certain to lead to success.

DON'T TAKE THE CABLE CAR UP MONTE BALDO IN AUGUST
The same holds true for any sunny summer days, holidays or long weekends. Unless you manage to catch the first car up, you might end up queuing for ages. Then, once you're at the top, you have to wait forever to go back down!

DO WEAR APPROPRIATE CLOTHING
It's fine for tourists to stroll along the narrow streets in T-shirt, shorts and sandals, but it's a real faux pas to sit down at a café table in swimming shorts.

DON'T TAKE THE CAR FOR SHORT JOURNEYS
You really only planned a short detour to Limone, but ended up spending the entire day in the car on the narrow Gardesana. It is often quicker to take the ferry.